THE OUTDOORSMAN'S GUIDE TO
WILDERNESS
CAMPING

THE OUTDOORSMAN'S GUIDE TO
WILDERNESS CAMPING

A complete manual for the adventurous camper,
including plans for tent making and camping in the snow.

by Douglas Durst

Pagurian Press

DUTTON

Library of Congress Catalog Card Number 78-18124
ISBN 0-525-04745-X
Printed and bound in Canada

for
Joanne

Contents

Acknowledgments

I would like to thank the many people who have supported the writing of this book. Some have offered a kind word of encouragement; others have provided helpful criticism; and still others have given valuable suggestions.

I wish to express a special thanks to Stuart Wilson, the man who sent me into the wilderness with small bands of greenhorns. As a leader, I learned to share with others the joys of wilderness camping.

My brother Larry provided his skills in the field of photography.

A special appreciation is due my wife, Joanne. She has been exceptionally thoughtful and helpful during the many hours spent writing this book.

The canoe pack takes just about everything anywhere but is not comfortable for long hauls.

Wilderness Camping 1

All of us have an appreciation of nature. Even the most ardent city dweller prefers natural woodgrain for his desk top and adorns his office with large potted plants and oils of spectacular mountains and violent seas.

We all enjoy books and pictures which depict nature's beauty. But it is even more spectacular actually being there. Although a lot of people pack their cars with camping equipment and head off for the wild country, they remain tied to their cars and therefore to roads. Their view of nature is limited to what can be seen from the roadside. But beyond those roads lie freedom and adventure. To experience it, the camper must leave his car and continue on foot — he can walk, ski, snowshoe, or paddle to land that has not been altered by man. Other forms of camping are restricted to easily accessible locations. Camping comforts — picnic tables, level tent sites, water, firewood, and latrines — are available for a fee. But roadside camping parks are overcrowded. Wilderness camping takes the camper beyond the parks into the real country.

Since all his provisions and equipment must be carried, he must be strong and fit. The weight and bulk of his gear must be minimal; gear is often specialized to attain minimum weight and bulk. Since only the absolute essentials can be taken along, little equipment is necessary. In fact, the average person probably has enough gear in his home to get started. A solid pack is essential; a tent and sleeping bag may also be essential (depending on where the camper intends to camp). But without question, wilderness camping is the cheapest way to camp.

Regions of uninhabited wilderness are all around us, and the pace of the trip can be adjusted so that children, even infants, can enjoy the experience.

What does the wilderness camper get for sacrificing modern conveniences and comforts? First, adventure. The country is new, and each day offers new experiences. The camper is called upon to be creative by living with limited resources. He must plan the trip, select the gear, and choose how to use that gear within a given environment. As he travels, he meets changing weather and terrain. He must rise to and meet those changes by adapting camping techniques.

Second, is natural beauty. There is so much to see, smell, hear, and touch.

Third, wilderness camping provides freedom. The camper is free from the restricting routines of modern life — paying bills, obeying traffic signs, and following a clock. He is free to choose where to camp, when to eat, and what to do. In the wilderness, the real person shines through. There is no need to put up a front.

Also, the exercise promotes good health. Although a camper is sometimes wet or cold, seldom does a cold or fever strike him while in the wilds.

And wilderness camping offers both a sense of community and of solitude. Camping with a small group of four to six develops a sense of unity and belonging. Yet there is also the opportunity for solitude.

Unfortunately many campers do not take full advantage of all that wilderness camping offers. They take the urban life with them into the back country. The wilderness is seen as an obstacle to be conquered, and they live in spite of rather than in harmony with the wilds, with the result that they return from a "campaign" exhausted, not refreshed.

Wilderness camping is simple, yet a challenge. This book has been written with both the tyro and the experienced camper in mind. To the inexperienced camper, it provides the knowledge necessary to enjoy our untouched lands. To the expert, it offers new suggestions. To the do-it-yourselfer, it includes simple plans for making equipment, including an entire tent.

The Plan 2

Planning a wilderness trip can be almost as exciting as the adventure itself. It starts with a dream. Imagination begins to tease your common sense and before you realize it, you have been bitten by the fever. You take concrete action by waterproofing your boots, studying maps, and checking the supply of freeze-dried foods at your local sporting-goods store. Soon you have blocked in your calendar with "camping" written over those special days or weeks. The success or failure of those days starts with planning. For the auto camper, planning is not critical. All one has to do is pack the car or trailer and roll away. If something has been forgotten, it can be bought in the nearest town. But wilderness camping does not include the convenience of a town plaza. Everything needed for the duration of the trip must be packed and carried. Only the essentials can be taken; all extras must be left behind.

BODY FITNESS

A trip into isolated land, when one is plagued with illness, stiff muscles, or fatigue is not an adventure but a nightmare. A weak body that complains at the activity is not just a nuisance but a safety hazard. I am not saying that to enjoy wilderness camping you must be a Charles Atlas or an Olympic athlete. But you should be reasonably fit and know when you have reached your physical limits. When you know your limits, you can plan the trip within your bounds for enjoyment and safety.

13

The only way to keep your body at a reasonable fitness level is to exercise it. Exercise is more than just strenuous activity: it is a frame of mind that becomes a lifestyle. In this frame of mind one chooses to walk to the store rather than drive, skip the elevator and walk those few flights of stairs, and pass up seconds at meals. And, if that frame of mind takes hold, it may even help the smoker put out his last cigaret.

Before you leave for your trip, "free" muscles that have been lazy. Three evenings a week do fifteen minutes of stretching exercises, such as toe-touching, sit-ups, and trunk bends. (Push-ups, chin-ups, and weight-lifting help increase the *strength* of muscles.)

To develop your respiratory and cardiovascular system, you must do strenuous activity. Exercising the respiratory system improves the volume and efficiency of your lungs. Improving the cardiovascular system strengthens your heart. A strong heart can pump more blood with less effort and has a longer life.

Enroll in a swimming class once a week, and jog for fifteen minutes another evening. Or play squash, bicycle, cross-country ski or do anything that leaves you breathless.

Here is a rough schedule that is easy to follow:

Monday   — 15 minutes of exercises
Tuesday   — swim class
Wednesday   — 15-minute run
Thursday   — 15 minutes of exercises
Saturday   — squash, golf, curling, or skiing

In three weeks you will notice considerable improvement in your body fitness.

The camping activity itself can be practiced before you leave. If you are backpacking, get out and walk. If you are canoe tripping, take a Sunday afternoon and paddle the lake in the town park.

MENTAL FITNESS

While you are toning your body, start to feed your mind. Drop into your local library and tell the librarian of your interests. He or she can show you how to find guidebooks, books on natural history, field guides, and books on camping. Guidebooks will give you ideas of what to see and a historical perspective of the region. The trip will be far more interesting if you know something of the area's past.

Natural history books explain the geological formations of the region and the biological relationships between plants and animals. The Peterson *Field Guides* are excellent for identifying and learning about the various species of wild plants and wildlife. Before I take groups into the back country, I find an hour or so of research in the library makes all trips more interesting and exciting.

Read other books on wilderness camping to broaden your knowledge. (See Bibliography on page 185.) You will probably borrow ideas from several books and use them to develop your own style. Even if you are an experienced camper, you can always learn something new.

One of the best ways to update your knowledge of the latest camping equipment is through catalogs. Send away for mail-order catalogs that specialize in outdoor activities. (They are usually available for the asking and often without a handling charge.) These catalogs are filled with the latest equipment and prices.

While you are flexing your mind, buy a compass and a map of your home region; then get out and practice. It is much better to get "lost" in your home neighborhood than somewhere in unfamiliar bush. *Be Expert with Map and Compass* by Kjellstrom is an excellent book to study.

While browsing at your sporting-goods store, ask for information about local outdoor clubs. Clubs specialize in backpacking, climbing, white-water canoeing, canoe tripping, orienteering, wildlife identification, and cross-country skiing. They may offer lectures, films, discussions, and outings. Members can help the novice choose equipment and advise him as to places to go and things to take.

FINDING A WILDERNESS

Vast regions in Canada and the United States are still uninhabited and are available to the wilderness-seeker. In Canada, the provinces control large areas of Crown land: parks and forest reserves that are open to the backpacker, skier, or canoeist. (Some areas require fire and travel permits.) Many provinces have established hiking trails and canoeing routes. Detailed information about these routes can be obtained by contacting the department or ministry in charge of parks at the capital of the province in which you are interested in camping.

For information regarding Canadian national parks write to:
The Canadian Office of Travel,
150 Kent Street, Ottawa, Canada K1A 0H6.

In the United States there are large national wilderness preserves, designated backpacking trails, and wild river preserves.

Write to: the United States Government Printing Office, Washington, D.C. 20402 for the following publications: *Search for Solitude*, which describes the National Wilderness Preservation System; *Trails for America*, which describes the National Scenic Trail System. (Two large trails, the Appalachian Trail and the Pacific Crest Trail, have already been established. Plans are afoot to create other backpacking trails.); *Public Access to Public Domain Lands*; *Backcountry Travel in the National Park System*; *National Forest Vacations*; *Our Public Lands* (a quarterly published by the Bureau of Land Management); *Backpacking in the National Forests*; and *Camping in National Parks*.

Get information on wild and scenic rivers by writing the Bureau of Outdoor Recreation, United States Department of the Interior, Washington, D.C. 20402; information on camping on forest industry land can be obtained by writing to the American Forest Institute, 1835 K St. N.W., Washington, D.C. 20006.

Other reliable sources of information on wilderness areas in *your* region can be found by contacting local wilderness clubs.

TOPOGRAPHICAL MAPS

Once you have decided where to go, buy detailed maps of the area. For wilderness camping, topographical maps are essential. The maps show buildings, roads, trails, streams, rivers, lakes, forest areas, clearings, and elevations. Changes in elevation are shown by a system of contour lines. A hiker would need a scale of about 1:62,500 or approximately one inch to a mile. Since a canoeist travels faster, often over open water, he may prefer a map with less detail such as a scale of 1:126,000 or one inch to two miles. Now you can plan your route and select potential campsites — and on the trip you will be able to follow the map with reference to visual landmarks — you will always know approximately where you are. The map does not, however, promise to show everything exactly as you had expected.

You can buy maps at outdoor or stationery stores, but they usually stock only regional maps. They will, however, order maps on request. Or, write:

in Canada:
Department of Mines and Technical Surveys,
Map Distribution Office,
615 Booth Street,
Ottawa, Ontario
K1A 0H6

east of the Mississippi:
U.S. Geological Survey,
1200 South Eads Street,
Arlington, Virginia
22202

west of the Mississippi:
U.S. Geological Survey,
Federal Center,
Denver, Colorado
80225

in Alaska:
U.S. Geological Survey,
520 Illinois Street,
Fairbanks, Alaska

Without a protective cover, any map soon becomes water-stained, and torn by wind and general use. A freezer bag with a zip-lock top makes an easy-to-use map case. With the map folded, it can be read from both sides, and the bag can be opened and closed many times before it begins to show signs of wear. It will keep the map clean, dry, and stiff for easy reading.

BEFORE LEAVING

Sit down and calculate a rough itinerary, using your maps. Figure an approximate starting time based on the time you rise in the morning and the travel time to your starting point. Estimate the campsites you expect to reach each day. Remember, poor weather may change your plans, so include at least one blow-over day. If you enjoy painting, drawing, photography, or even writing poetry, you may wish to devote some time just for that. Or, you may wish to spend time just relaxing and enjoying the beauty around you. It is your trip, so include in it the activities you enjoy.

After you have calculated an itinerary, notify a friend of your plans and expected return date. In the event of a mishap, your friend can tell the authorities roughly where you are. (He may also be kind enough to pick up your mail and water your plants.)

Depending on the area, you may need a fire permit or a fishing license. Check the necessary requirements.

In some areas, especially in isolated regions, notify police and forest authorities of your itinerary. While in these regions, it is comforting to know you have a few friends on the outside.

To avoid a last-minute rush, draw up a checklist under these headings: Food, Cooking and Camping Equipment, Clothing, Shelter, Toiletries, and Miscellaneous.

Below is a checklist for a two-week canoe trip.

Food
14 breakfasts
14 lunches
14 suppers
salt and pepper
powdered milk
sugar
coffee/tea
hot chocolate
drink mix (Kool-Aid, Tang, etc.)
cooking oil
trail snacks

Cooking and Camping Equipment
pots (2)
frying pan
plates/cups (one for each person)
eating utensils
tin foil
grill (optional)
stove/fuel
spatula/spoon
garden trowel
nylon rope
matches

Shelter
tent or tarp
pegs
sleeping bag
foam pad (optional)
packs

Canoeing Equipment
canoe
paddles
tuck tape (for patching)
life jackets

Clothing
socks
underwear
pyjamas or long johns (optional)
T-shirt
trousers
shirt — cotton
shirt — wool

windbreaker
raingear
hat
swimsuit
sneakers
boots (optional)
sun glasses

Miscellaneous
first-aid kit
matches
maps and compass
survival kit
flashlight (optional)
notebook and pen
camera and film (optional)
fire permit (if applicable)

Toiletries
toothbrush
toothpaste
soap
toilet paper
towel (optional)
sanitary supplies (optional)
mirror (optional)

For a two-week backpacking trip, you obviously would not need the canoe but you should add a canteen and boots. A winter camper should add a down-filled jacket with an insulated hood. Mitts and thermal underwear and socks would also be added. Naturally, winter campers do not need sneakers and bathing suits. Since during the winter it becomes dark early, a flashlight is an asset.

Before you pack, lay everything out on the floor. Go through your checklist carefully, ticking off each item. Review each item and its contribution to the trip. If you are backpacking, keep in mind that the average carrying weight is about 16 kg. (35 lbs.). Some people may wish to carry more, others less. On a canoe trip, with portages, you can take a heavier load without too much difficulty. If everything is checked and accounted for, you are ready to pack.

DROP OUTS

Sometimes, just as your anticipation has reached its highest level, the phone rings and the other half of your trip explains that, for some reason beyond his control, he cannot go with you. Should you go or cancel your plans? Because of the nature of wilderness camping, it is foolish to go alone.

I once spent a year planning a three-week trip for eight. When the time came to collect the shopping money, six had dropped out. The trip was restricted to two — my brother and me. We went. So be flexible — if there are two of you, I say "go" and ask your drop-out to water your plants.

The Essential Tools   3

Wilderness camping requires some tools to make the experience more natural and less of an ordeal. Some campers get hooked on the latest fads in camping equipment and spend a great deal of cash on unnecessary gadgets, but wilderness camping does not allow a lot of convenient extras. When you stop to think, the simplicity of camping is one of its joys — why clutter it up?

The tools you take must be light, have minimal bulk, and be multi-functional. A specialized tool that performs one job is an unnecessary burden.

THE KNIFE

Knives, for some unknown reason, have a special mystique which often obscures their real purpose. Presented with an expensive selection of sparkling blades, it is easy to forget our common sense. I have seen more than one camper march into the bush wielding a knife vicious enough to halt the charge of a grizzly but ridiculous and downright dangerous cutting open a package of noodle soup.

The questions we face when buying a knife are: How big? What type? There are two types of knives to consider: a hunting knife complete with a carrying sheath, and a simple folding knife. I must confess, that my knife is not ideal: in my teens I was given a good hunting knife with a six-inch blade. Along the blade runs a blood groove for easier skinning of a deer (at least that is what they say; I've never skinned a deer). My knife is too large; if you plan to buy a sheath knife, spend your money on a good, small one. A good knife holds its edge longer; the handle remains tighter; and the sheath has a longer life. Don't waste your money on a cheap knife.

A simple garden trowel is small and lightweight and has a 1001 uses.

My knife is a moderately expensive Solingen; other good knives are: Buck, Browning, Colt, Gerber, Olsen, and Puma. Some cheaper knives (but still good quality) are: Case, Marble, Normark, Schrade-Walden, Western, and Russell. Ruka knives import a variety of blade qualities from different manufacturers. They offer a broad selection and try to stock something for everyone.

A good folding or pocket knife is also suitable. It will last a long time and is not expensive. Look for a smooth spring action as the blade folds into the handle. It should lock into both the opened and closed positions. When closed, the point of the blade must be protected by both sides of the handle. When opened, the blade must be secure and not wobble. Cutting usually involves packages of soup, rope, fish, sticks, and thousands of other hand-held objects. A blade between three and four inches long will do most of these jobs. Any larger and the knife is no longer a pocket knife. Get a knife with a chain ring to hook on to your belt; you will never lose it.

Some knives come with all kinds of gadgets. Personally, I prefer a simple Swiss Army knife with only a blade.

A hunting knife (with a sheath), a folding pocket knife, and carborundum stone (for touch-ups) are all the cutting tools a wilderness camper needs.

SHARPENING

A dull knife is an accident looking for a place to happen; it's dangerous. A dull blade requires more strength to cut; the increase in pressure increases the chances of slipping. A wound from a dull knife is worse than one from a sharp blade, because a dull blade tears the flesh rather than slices it. Either way, it is a messy business, so keep your blade sharp and use it wisely.

Cheap knives use a softer metal and are easier to sharpen, but they lose their edge more quickly. If the edge is ruined, only an oilstone supported on a table or bench can replace it. The stone should have a fine and a medium side. Add some light machine oil to the medium side first. The oil will float away metal particles and prevent the pores of the stone from getting clogged. Place the blade at a 20-degree angle and stroke the blade across the stone so that your finished stroke reaches the blade's point. Change sides with each stroke. As the blade moves, apply firm, consistent pressure. With a little practice, you'll find the task will develop into a reflex action.

23

The knife may form a wire edge (a tiny bead develops running down the length of the blade). This wire edge will break away the first time you use the knife, or, you may wish to strop it off on a piece of leather strap or belt. I use the palm of my hand. Draw the blade backwards on each side a few times. The blade should now be sharp enough to shave with. To touch up an edge, the procedure is the same except light pressure is applied.

Carry a pocket carborundum stone for quick touch-ups in the bush, where a little spit substitutes for oil.

THE AX AND HATCHET

An ax is not necessary in wilderness camping. It may have its place in a stationary camp where logs must be split, but in the wild country, an ax is heavy and unnecessary. To use one safely takes months of careful practice, and an isolated campsite is not the place to learn. An accident can happen too easily; why not avoid it entirely?

Wood for fires should not be chopping-size when there is plenty of smaller, thumb-sized wood available; tent pegs can be hammered in with a medium-sized stone.

One summer, I worked as a canoe out-tripper in a camping program for emotionally disturbed adolescents. These kids had pronounced emotional problems making it difficult for them to vent their feelings conventionally. Periodically, someone would "blow" as his temper went out of control. From then on I preferred not to have axes or hatchets around. And I've never missed them since. The saving in bulk, weight, cost, and safety has far outweighed their convenience.

A GARDEN TROWEL

Camping shovels, even the so-called compact models, are bulky and heavy and an added expense. I've found that a simple garden trowel does as well. It's light and easy to pack — perfect for digging latrines, cleaning a fireplace, and digging the occasional rain trough around the tent. (Take care to replace all sod and leave the location just as you found it. Please, do not use your trowel to bury your garbage; carry it out.)

A PLASTIC OR RUBBERIZED SHEET

My 9′×9′ plastic sheet has many uses — I have punched grommets in its corners and sides, therefore I can tie it up anywhere. I use it as a firewood cover, a rainfly, and a ground sheet. In an emergency, it can be a warm, dry lean-to shelter. It has covered me and my equipment many times during brief thunderstorms. In areas of moderate or heavy rainfall, a plastic sheet is indeed useful. Better even than a plastic sheet is a polyethylene tarp. These heavy duty tarps are fiber reinforced. They come with grommets and ropes on each corner. A tarp 6′×8′ costs $11.50; a 12′×14′ costs $25.00.

CANTEEN

A canteen is a must for all hikers, climbers, and backpackers. Desert canteens are usually made of lightweight steel and can be bought in two or four-quart sizes. The straps are designed to be carried over the shoulder. G1 type and Scout canteens are smaller, made of aluminum or even plastic. If the area is arid, the larger desert canteen is a better investment.

ROPE

Very often you need to tie something with a strong piece of rope, either to string up food to avoid tempting the bears, make a shelter or fly, or tow a canoe. For lining canoes through rough water, 50 feet of 1/4-inch nylon rope with 1,200x1,800 lbs. capacity is sufficient. Backpackers and cross-country skiers do not need anything stronger than 1/8-inch nylon rope. Nylon does not stretch like hemp, and a simple match will melt the ends to prevent fraying. It won't rot or mildew. (I store mine in the trunk of my car.)

A compass and first-aid kit are also essential, but they are discussed in the **Direction** and **Safety** chapters.

COMMON-SENSE CARE

Use your head and care for your equipment. Don't leave your tools lying around where someone could step on or trip over them. Knives and hatchets will rust if not kept clean and dry. The handle on your trowel or hatchet could attract the nibbling teeth of a salt-hungry porcupine, so keep them tucked away. Keep your rope properly coiled to prevent kinks weathering and damaging it. The small investment you have made in equipment will give years of safe, dependable service, but remember that the responsibility of caring for it is yours.

The Sleeping Bag

4

Getting enough rest and good food are vital to the success of a wilderness trip. Without these, nothing can prevent the trip from turning into an ordeal. A rain-soaked day can be faced with a grin if you know that a hot dinner and cozy bed are waiting for you at the end of it.

A sleeping bag is the wilderness camper's most critical purchase. Sleeping bags come in a confusing variety of insulations, shapes, and construction techniques. First consider the type of camping you plan to do and how much you can afford to spend. Buy the bag in a reputable store — you are sure then of getting the quality you pay for. If you are serious about wilderness camping, pay a minimum of $70 for a down-filled bag; winter camping requires a bag that costs twice that amount.

Some reputable manufacturers are: Woods, Browning, Bauer, and Reid. There are other fine bag manufacturers, so read this chapter carefully, then shop around.

INSULATION

The main purpose of insulation is to trap the air around the body and prevent it from circulating. Without air circulation, heat cannot easily leave the body and dissipate into the surrounding air. Therefore the body's natural heat is conserved. Since the camper must carry this insulation, he must consider its weight and bulk. The insulation must be able to trap air, but it must also allow moisture released from the body to escape.

Down

The best material is natural goose-down. It is exceptionally light and compresses into an unimaginable size — six hundred cubic inches packs down to a volume of fifteen cubic inches. In minutes it can be fluffed back to its original volume, even after it has been compressed for long periods of time. Air clings to the tiny down fibers, and air circulation is stopped.

Goose-down is superior to duck-down. Down from countries in northern climates, such as Canada, the northern United States, and northern Europe, is superior to down from southern climates. In Asian countries the warm climate prevents the birds from developing their thickest and fluffiest down.

Feather insulation is not as efficient as down. Feathers occasionally poke their stems through the nylon and jab the sleeper as he rolls.

With care, a good bag will last a long time. I bought a used down bag seven years ago. Each summer I practically live in it and it still has many seasons left.

Dacron Fiberfill II

Unfortunately, some people are allergic to down. For them, the next-best option is Dacron Fiberfill II. It is definitely a second choice; but, it will not rot or mildew, is less expensive than down, and can be easily drycleaned. A dacron bag is suitable for summer camping only, when the nights are not too cold.

Kapok

Kapok is the insulation used in the cheapest bags (and in some life jackets). A fiber extracted from the seed-pods of trees from southeast Asia, it is cheap and very bulky. As insulation, two quality wool blankets are a better investment.

Sleeping Bag Shapes

The *mummy bag* offers maximum warmth and is compact. It is the best bag for the mountaineer or the winter camper. Some people, however, feel it resembles a straitjacket and they cannot rest in it properly. Mummy bags are long; the better ones have a hood with a drawstring. Since twenty per cent of body heat is lost through the head, a hood is necessary in cold weather.

A rectangular down sleeping bag.

Barrel bags are shaped like a barrel. They taper at the feet and head and bulge in the middle. They roll into a compact bundle but some find them uncomfortable unless flat on their backs or curled into the fetal ball.

My wife and I own two *rectangular bags* that can be zipped together. (Some other shapes also can be zipped together.) The bags are well over 6 feet long and about 34 inches wide. If you are a large person, you may wish to invest in a wider bag. Alone or zipped together, these bags leave plenty of room for tossing and turning without twisting the bag and yourself into a pretzel.

When you buy clothes, you assert your rights and try them on first. Do the same thing when buying a bag. Take off your shoes and crawl into the bag. Stretch and roll over to get some feeling for the bag. You may find that a smaller bag will be just as comfortable, or, you may want a larger one. Trying it first is the only way to be sure.

29

SHELL CONSTRUCTION OF SLEEPING BAGS

The shell can be made of synthetic and cotton blends or of pure nylon. Some people prefer an inner shell of 100 percent nylon. I find it feels cold, so have an inner material in a cotton blend. Nylon must be of a rip-stop type, especially with down insulation, otherwise a tiny hole will spread, and soon you will have down everywhere. Also, the nylon must be tightly woven to ensure that the down does not pop through the pores in the material.

CUT CONSTRUCTION

Do not be confused by the on-going battle of cut constructions. Differential cuts have an inner shell that is smaller than the outer shell. The principle is that if you press an elbow or knee against the inside, you will not touch the outside; therefore, you will not tamper with the insulation. The problem with this theory is that since the inner shell is smaller, it is being constantly stretched, thereby creating air pockets around your body. In a space-filler cut bag, the inside shell hangs loosely around the body and therefore reduces the air pockets.

BAFFLE CONSTRUCTION

Baffles are the pockets of down created by sewn pieces of cloth or netting. They keep the down from moving around inside the shell. Otherwise, all the down would soon collect at the feet. Baffles can be doughnut-shaped and run around you, or, in a checker-board pattern. There are five different baffle-construction methods. The simplest construction has the same seam straight through from the outside to the inside, and cold air can pass through since there is no insulation along the seam: it feels as though one is being branded with cold air in the pattern of the seams. Avoid this baffle construction: buy a bag where the outside seam is separated by cloth or netting from the inside seam.

Winter camping may require a bag that has laminated baffles. Overlapping baffles hold the down in place, and these are the most expensive bags.

LOFT

Loft is the thickness of the bag when it is fluffed up. As the loft increases, the bag increases in warmth. Bags range in loft from about four to twelve inches. A bag with 1½ lbs. of down will have about four inches of loft — good for a minimum temperature of about +5°C or 40°F (late spring, summer, and early fall). The chart below shows how loft varies with weight and approximate minimum temperature.

Loft (in inches)	Weight (in pounds)	Minimum Temperature
4	1½	+5C (+40 F)
6	2	−12C (+10 F)
12	3	−29C (−20 F)

The figures are somewhat deceptive — as the loft underneath is compressed by the body, it has less of an insulating effect. Also, temperature tolerances vary between individuals.

THE ZIPPER

If anything goes wrong with your bag it probably will be the zipper. Forget metal zippers. They freeze, break, and jam. If you happen to lean your bare back against one, a cold shock will wake you. Nylon zippers are an improvement over metal, but they can still break. There is no perfect zipper.

The zipper should be a reasonable size for strength and durability. It should zip to the bottom as well as to the top to keep cool on warm nights. A down-filled flap should cover the zipper, otherwise a cool draft will blow in.

My old mummy bag does not have a zipper. To air it out, the bag must be pulled inside-out, which is not as effective as opening it completely. Mummy bags *are* available that zip to the bottom — a help in getting in and out of them and in airing the bags.

SEW-IT-YOURSELF SLEEPING BAG

You can save about fifty percent of the cost by sewing your own bag from Frostline kits (452 Burbank, Broomfield, Col. 80020). The kits arrive complete with the materials ready to sew. Clear directions are included, the only skill required is to sew a straight line. The down is pre-pocketed and labelled so that after the compartments are sewn, the down is simply pushed in, and you are assured of the right amount of down per compartment. Frostline kits are also available for tents, jackets, packs, and other camping accessories.

For occasional summer trips, a blanket bag can easily be made out of two warm blankets. Fold each blanket in half and tuck one blanket inside the other with the folds on opposite sides. Fold the bottom over and pin around the edges. To get into the bag, crawl in from the top — it is like slipping into a giant envelope.

A PILLOW

A pillow is an extravagance on a wilderness trip. You can get along with substitutes. Stuff a sweater or a jacket into a sleeping-bag sack. On a canoe trip, kapok lifejackets do the job, but they have a habit of getting wet.

CARE OF THE SLEEPING BAG

If you are using your bag without a tent or tent floor, place a waterproof ground sheet under the bag, otherwise damp will penetrate and increase the chance of tearing or damaging the nylon shell.

If a spark pops from the fire, nylon will melt, leaving a 2-inch hole. Never lay the bag near a fire, or attempt to dry a wet bag by the fire — it is not worth the risk.

A long life for the bag is ensured by keeping it clean. Whenever possible during and after the trip, air the bag in the sun. The sun will naturally clean and disinfect it. Some people claim that a down bag can be drycleaned, if a weaker cleaning solution is used. These cleaning solutions, however, remove the natural oils in the down, and a strong solution will ruin its insulating properties. Personally, I feel that drycleaning is an unnecessary risk. Also, the agitators on top-loading machines are murderous on the delicate baffle construction. Spots can be washed off using soap and water, or the entire bag can be put into the bathtub. Warm water, with a non-detergent soap, such as Ivory or Sunlight, will remove the dirt. Soak, wash, and rinse the bag right in the tub. Do not wring the water out by twisting; squeeze out the excess water. After washing, lay the wet bag flat — if it is hung, the down will cluster at one end of its baffle. It is safe to put the bag into a dryer set at *warm* for a couple of cycles. For a finishing touch, give the bag a day or two of fresh air and sun.

As the bag is drying, check it for rips. (On your next trip you will feel foolish trying to mend a broken zipper in the dark on the first night out.)

To keep the down fluffy, bags should be stored decompressed. Ideally, they should be hung full length in your closet. If your closet space is limited, the fluffed bags can be stored in a box under a bed.

Never attempt to waterproof your bag. The chemicals will damage the down, and stop the flow of body moisture through the nylon. The result? Cold nights spent lying in your own cold perspiration. When I was a teenager, I placed a plastic sheet on top of my bag one night. In the morning I accused my buddies of playing tricks. I thought they had soaked the top of my bag with water.

INSULATING PADS

Except for winter camping, an insulating pad is a luxury. Even rough ground does not inhibit my sleep after a busy day but some people have a legitimate problem sleeping on the cold, rough ground.

The worst kind of padding is an air mattress. As you move on it, the air inside circulates; hence, there is little insulation from the ground. Also, the mattress must be inflated, which can be an exhausting task for your lungs, or blown up with a pump that must be carried. Once blown to the right softness, however, the mattress is quite comfortable. Uninflated, a rubberized mattress weighs a ton and is bulky. For wilderness tripping, leave the air mattress at the pool for the kids.

Synthetic pads provide excellent insulation, but polyurethane mattresses have open cells which make them bulky. They are best left in the back of the stationwagon at the cottage. For the wilderness, a closed-celled, ensolite pad is best. It has an uneven or ridged underside, but is smooth on the top. It rolls up tightly and provides good insulation for its ¹/₂-inch to 1¹/₂-inch thickness, and will make stony ground quite comfortable. To save volume, a four-foot length will pad your body — legs do not lose very much heat and do not need padding. The pad absorbs moisture like a sponge, so cover it. Sew a cover, using waterproof nylon for the bottom and cotton for the top. The cotton top will prevent you from sliding around while sleeping. The pad should be rolled with the waterproof side out, to keep rain out while carrying it.

Forget the classic woodsman's trick of cutting a mattress of evergreen boughs — with so many trippers entering the bush, there is not enough time for the forest to regenerate itself. Also, the campsite is left in an ugly mess with scarred trees and browning branches on the ground.

To get a little extra insulation, lay out your day clothes under your sleeping bag. Also, a space blanket will reduce heat-loss by radiation. This large, foil ground sheet folds into a tiny package which can be spread on the tent floor. It also has many emergency uses, for example, as a temporary shelter.

NIGHTCLOTHES

If you have a good sleeping bag, it is best to dress lightly. A T-shirt will absorb your body oils and prevent them from collecting on the bag, and the bag will stay cleaner longer.

If you must dress at night change your clothes both before going to bed and before rising the following morning. Why? Because the moisture released by your body during the night will cool when you leave your bag, and in your damp clothes, the mornings will seem colder than they really are.

For cold nights, a warm pair of wool socks are cozy. If you still wake with cold feet, pull an empty packsack over the bottom of the bag.

Camping Clothes 5

Camping clothes have two major functions. One, to protect the body surface from sunburn, insects, scrapes, and cuts; two, to conserve body heat when the air is cold, and to ventilate heat away when the air is warm.

Our bodies must maintain an internal temperature of 37°C (98.6°F). Air moving across the skin accounts for 60 to 70 percent of body-heat loss. Blood circulates the heat. When the body begins to overheat, blood vessels at the body's surface expand (vasodilation), and the heat moves from the organs to the skin and then is released to the air. When the body begins to cool, the blood vessels constrict (vasoconstriction) to reduce blood flow to the skin surface. Heat is conserved for the vital organs. The restricted circulation causes the extremities (hands and feet) to feel the cold first. Temperature tolerances, however, vary with each individual — you know your limits better than anyone.

The camper must have the *minimum* amount of clothing for the expected changes in temperature. Summer in high altitudes will have a wide temperature range. Nights will be cold, days will warm up and could get hot. Remember, every item taken into the wilderness must have a use. There is no room for extra clothing. Each piece must be evaluated in terms of weight and bulk and it must be practical. The fashionable and attractive must come second to the rugged, durable, and warm.

To meet a wide temperature range without excess weight and bulk, there is only one approach to take — the layer method. Five different layers are worn or removed, depending on the air temperature and one's degree of physical activity.

FIRST LAYER: UNDERWEAR

For men, undershorts should fit loosely for comfort. Especially when backpacking, any underwear that causes minor rubbing will worsen as the day goes on. Nylon shorts dry faster than cotton, but cotton may be more comfortable. One extra pair is all that is needed.

A cotton T-shirt can be used as an undershirt for warmth. On hot days, it can be worn alone. In the event of an accident, a T-shirt can be made into a sling, compress, or bandage. Also, the T-shirt reduces friction from pack straps and prevents sunburn. Carrying a pack over a tender sunburn is torturous.

SECOND LAYER: PANTS AND SHIRT

Tight pants are uncomfortable. They are more resistant to body movement and the friction that results is wasted energy. It could also result in raw patches of skin. Loose pants should be worn, for example, full-cut jeans. Jeans have a tight weave that resists snagging and tearing and protects the legs from scratches, insects, and sunburn. New jeans need to be broken in. Once through the washer will soften them. Cuffs are a nuisance, since they hook easily on plants and fill with dirt. A slight flare in the pant leg is convenient for covering the boot. Some campers like woollen pants, but I find them too heavy, particularly when they are wet.

Fashion has brought knickers back and knickers are now popular among cross-country skiers who wear them with long woollen socks. Climbers also find them comfortable and durable since many pairs come with double seats.

A tight-weave pair of shorts is great for hiking on hot days. On a canoe trip, a simple bathing suit may be more convenient.

Since weight is most important for the backpacker, take only one pair of pants. Weight is less important for the canoeist and he will feel more secure if he knows that he has an extra dry pair.

A camping shirt should have long sleeves for protection against sunburn and insects. In bug country, a long shirttail tightly tucked in is a must. Look for a shirt with a tight weave of blended cotton (polyester and cotton). The shirt should be a little loose so that a T-shirt can be worn underneath without binding. Breast pockets with button flaps are handy for carrying small items.

Rainwear to fit your budget. On the left is an inexpensive plastic coat; on the right is a nylon-rubberized rain suit—both will do the job.

THIRD LAYER: LONG-SLEEVED SWEATER

A lightweight turtleneck with a tight weave is popular among some campers. Personally, the necks bother me; I stick to my favorite, a hooded sweatshirt. The inside is soft and cozy and it can be worn over a shirt or next to the skin. Rather than abuse a new sweater you might try used clothing stores. They generally have a variety in the right price range.

FOURTH LAYER: JACKET

Depending on your body metabolism and where you camp, you may be able to skip this layer. But, during summer camping in northern Canada, a wool jacket is ideal. It is actually a heavy shirt made from 100 per cent wool. When too warm, the front can be unbuttoned and the sleeves rolled up. It's a little bulky, but provides insulation even when wet. Wash by hand in cool water and hang to dry.

FIFTH LAYER: WINDBREAKER

This layer is essential for all wilderness camping. The windbreaker reduces heat loss from convection (moving air). A nylon jacket is light, compact, and inexpensive. Many come with a hood. Or, wear a rubberized rain jacket.

RAINWEAR

Some areas get so little rain that rainwear is unnecessary. Yet, it seems that when you leave it behind, that is when you need it the most.

A two-piece rain suit made of rubberized nylon is the best buy — the jacket can be worn as a windbreaker. The cheap plastic suits rip easily but with care can last through a couple of camping seasons. The suits are cold against the skin so you may wish to wear a long-sleeved shirt underneath. The major problem with these suits is that they do not breathe; hence moisture builds up inside. Sometimes I am as wet inside the suit as the weather is outside.

A simple plastic raincoat is cheap but effective. A poncho is another economical solution. It is basically a ground sheet with a hole and hood for the head. Plastic ponchos come in bright colors; you may have seen children wearing them on rainy school days. Army-surplus ponchos are heavily rubberized and last for years. Ponchos have better ventilation than raincoats. They also can be used as a ground sheet, to cover firewood, or as an emergency shelter. Some ponchos are designed to cover your pack as well. But on windy days, they do little but flap around.

Whatever you decide to get for rainwear, be sure to pack it where it can be easily reached. The first time you are caught in a flash storm, you will feel silly groping for your poncho with your gear half-unpacked.

HATS

A lot of campers neglect their heads. I love a hat and wear one all the time in the outdoors. Mine fits snuggly and keeps my hair out of my eyes. The brim is wide enough to cut the sun's glare but is not wide enough to catch every breeze and blow off. In hot weather, a dunking in water changes it into a portable air conditioner. In cold weather, it helps keep my head warm. Around the fire, it does duty as a quick pot-holder. While I am fishing, it keeps my lures out of the way. I even squirt bug juice on it to keep the mosquitoes away. Camping would not be the same without my battered hat.

Some campers wear a bandana around their neck — as a sweatband, handkerchief, quick bandage, pot-holder, or whatever.

WINTER CAMPING: SPECIAL NEEDS

Besides staying warm, the winter camper must stay dry. Wet clothes absorb vital body heat very quickly, creating a dangerous situation. Winter clothing requirements follow the same principles as summer clothing — the five-layer method is the basis of sensible winter camping.

Underwear made of an open fishnet material is the most efficient. The tiny pockets trap the warm air inside and allow perspiration to evaporate. However, an outer shirt must be worn to allow the thermal principle to work. Long johns are another good first layer for people who feel the cold. But if you perspire easily, you may find that they get damp. In damp underwear, you are worse off than in none.

39

Some campers like wool pants and shirts as the second layer. Then a tight weave has excellent insulating properties. (I prefer a comfortable cotton shirt since the wool irritates my skin.)

Over the shirt, a heavy fisherman's knit sweater or a tightly woven ski sweater is best, preferably a turtleneck.

Another layer can be added before the jacket — polyester or down-filled vest. Down is better, but either helps conserve vital body heat.

For the fourth layer, nothing is better than a quality down-filled jacket or parka. The same principles apply to down jackets or parkas as to the sleeping bags described in the previous chapter. Quality goose-down contained in a nylon shell is the best. It compresses easily, breathes by allowing moisture to escape, and offers great insulation. About $1^1/2$ inches of loft is adequate. A nylon zipper with dome snaps on a wind flap cuts out the wind. Good jackets and parkas have overlapping down baffles. The overlapping reduces drafts entering through the seams. Wear a snug down-filled collar and nylon hood on the neck and head. Some parkas have fur trim around the hood edge to reduce the force of the wind around the face. A drawstring at the base of the coat eliminates drafts up the back.

There are, however, two problems with down jackets and parkas: one, when wet they provide little insulation, and two, a spark from a fire is sure to melt a hole in the nylon shell. (Some parkas use a cotton-nylon blend which helps reduce this hazard.)

Wash a down jacket or parka the same way as a sleeping bag.

You can make your own jacket using a Frostline kit. These kits come in a variety of styles, cuts, and sizes.

When shopping for a jacket or parka, go to reputable outdoor stores. Prices range between $80 and $200. Remember, you get what you pay for.

If you get cold easily, buy a knee-length parka. These trap the warm air around the thighs and help reduce heat loss. The disadvantage is they are heavy and bulky, hence are not suitable for mountain climbing or vigorous activity.

The effectiveness of a hat or hood in keeping the body warm is often underestimated. About 20 per cent of heat-loss is through the head. Since the brain needs a constant flow of fresh blood, your body cannot totally restrict the flow to the head and therefore there is a continual heat loss. The old saying is true: if your feet are cold, put on your hat.

When not wearing my hood, I don my favorite wool tuque. In cold weather, it can be rolled down to cover the ears; in warmer weather it can be rolled to rest on top of the head.

In extreme cold, a face mask prevents the face from freezing. A beard is a slight complication. Breath moisture freezes the beard to the mask, so take your time removing the mask.

Winter camping demands another protective accessory — dark glasses. The sun reflects off the snow, creating a damaging glare. Dark glasses are a must. In a pinch, emergency glasses can be made by cutting a slit in cardboard or birch bark and tying it around the head. Snow blindness is discussed in Chapter 17.

Remember, temperature alone does not dictate how cold it really is. Humidity and wind are other factors. The chart below shows the effectiveness of wind in absorbing your body heat:

Thermometer Temperature °F

Wind Velocity in M.P.H.	30	25	20	15	10	-5	-0	-5	-10	-15	-20	-25	-30	-35	-40	-45
10	20	14	8	2	-4	-10	-15	-21	-27	-33	-39	-45	-50	-56	-62	-68
15	13	7	0	-6	-12	-18	-25	-31	-38	-44	-50	-57	-63	-69	-75	-81
20	8	2	-5	-12	-19	-25	-32	-39	-45	-52	-59	-66	-72	-79	-85	-92
25	5	-2	-9	-17	-24	-30	-37	-44	-51	-58	-65	-72	-78	-86	-93	-99
30	3	-5	-12	-20	-27	-33	-41	-48	-55	-63	-70	-77	-83	-91	-96	-104
35	0	-7	-14	-22	-29	-36	-44	-51	-58	-66	-73	-81	-87	-95	-102	-109
40	-1	-9	-18	-24	-31	-38	-46	-53	-61	-69	-76	-84	-91	-98	-105	-112

(Flesh may freeze within 1 minute).

To find the wind-chill factor, read across from the known wind velocity to below the current temperature. The shaded area represents temperatures at which skin freezes.

Boots: Your Foundation   6

Blistered or cold feet can ruin the pleasure of a wilderness trip. Hiking into the bush in poorly fitted boots results in walking out of it in pain. Unless you are a masochist, you should pay attention to the messages your feet are sending you and treat them accordingly. There is no last word on foot care for the wilderness camper; it depends very much on your type of camping and your personal preferences. Foot needs for the backpacker are different than those for the canoe tripper and different again for the winter camper; how much you wish to spend will also affect your decision.

SOCKS

Few things relieve a tired pair of feet more than warm, dry socks. By keeping another pair handy, you can change into a clean pair at rest stops. Some campers prefer to wear two pairs of socks. Next to the skin, they wear a thin, soft, cotton pair and then, on top, a thicker wool or wool-blended sock. The thicker sock absorbs the moisture released by feet and also acts as a soft cushion. Cotton socks alone get wet too quickly. In cold weather, heavy work socks made of wool are good, but thermal ski socks are best.

HIKING AND BACKPACKING

Buying a pair of boots can be a big investment. To avoid this cost, a light walking shoe can help get you started. *Desert boots* or *wallabees* are great for day hikes or short backpacking trips. The crepe soles are fair shock absorbers and the soft leather is comfortable but not fragile.

    For hiking without stiff climbing, light work or hunting boots, such as made by Durham and Greb, measure up well. The crepe soles absorb the shock but the lack of deep tread makes climbing on rough terrain difficult. They are, however, less damaging to delicate grasses and plants than hiking boots. When buying work boots, remember that steel toes are extra weight and avoid them unless you plan to use your boots primarily for work. Buy boots without seams on the toe — extra seams can become uncomfortable after a day's hiking.

Hiking boots come in three different categories. Light, medium, or heavy boots are designed for hiking, hiking with some climbing, and climbing, respectively. Hiking boots do not make very good climbing boots and vice versa. Light boots have a comfortable leather shoe on a soft sole and are ideal for most backpacking. Climbing boots have a stiff shoe with thick, stiff soles with deep cleats. Some campers become fanatics about weight and buy only super-light tent poles, then purchase the heaviest clompers that they can find — and a few ounces saved on their backs are lost by the "space" boots they are forced to lift with each step.

Look for *Vibram* on the soles.

Vibram, an Italian manufacturer, makes most of the soles for better-quality boots. Other brand names to look out for are: Dunham, Danner, Pivetta, Vasque, and Eddie Bauer. For a light hiking boot, you can expect to pay between $25 and $35. Slightly heavier boots cost between $5 and $10 more. Always shop in a reputable store — you will get your money's worth.

If boots are more than six inches high, they will probably rub your leg or restrain the movement of your ankle. A padded tongue helps. Padding along the top of the boot is designed to keep out sand and also aids in comfort. Speed lacing is handy, but a good fit is most important. Rawhide lacing looks wild, but because they stretch, nylon braided laces are a better deal. If you have trouble keeping your feet warm, pay a little more and buy insulated boots.

It has recently become fashionable to wear hiking-type boots, and hiking boot look-alikes are sold everywhere. These "cool" boots are not bargains. If you buy a pair, keep them for around the house.

Before you buy a pair of boots, trim your toe nails so that you can get an accurate fit. Take your favorite pair of socks along, too. Sizes vary; your normal size may not apply to boots. Remember, if the boot is hurting in the store, it will hurt worse after hiking all day. The boot must feel snug and hold the heel firmly. In a good fit, there

Moccasins with fluffy down-filled socks are ideal for winter camping.

should be no pressure points. Keep trying on boots until you find a pair that feels just right.

Ordering by mail can have disastrous results. But if you must, send a tracing of your feet with socks on. When the boots arrive, try them on inside and, if they don't fit, send them back with an explanation of why they fit poorly.

Breaking in a new pair of boots on the trail can be painful: before the trail, walk to the store, to work, anywhere, to put on some mileage. This will soften and stretch the leather. Increase the distance until your boots still feel comfortable after an extended walk.

CANOEING

Footwear for the canoeist is different from that for the hiking backpacker. Wearing heavy boots in a canoe or kayak is inviting trouble — they could damage the fragile frame of a kayak and their weight would be dangerous in a capsize. For canoe tripping, a pair of light

Sturdy work boots are more than adequate for most camping. Mukluks are warm and comfortable to wear around the campsite.

running shoes with soft soles can be worn both in the canoe and out, gripping wet logs and rocks. Hiking boots would be ideal for long portages but lacing them and taking them off is a nuisance on short portages. Every portage seems to have a wet mud hole impossible to negotiate around; hiking boots take a long time to dry and too many dunkings ruin them. Low-cut sneakers can get pulled off just when the going is the roughest; ankle-height basketball shoes are best. Carry a spare pair to wear around camp while your day pair is drying out.

Joanne, my wife, prefers good-quality deck shoes. They have strong supporting arches that can be removed for quick drying. The soles are excellent for absorbing shocks and for gripping on wet surfaces.

WINTER CAMPING

To about -12° C, an insulated pair of work boots with heavy wool socks keeps feet warm. Cozy leather mukluks with a fur lining are also good. Sheepskin lining makes the insides very warm. Skidoo boots or laced rubber boots with thick felt innersoles are comfortable for around camp but not for hiking.

A cross-country skier or snowshoer may prefer a light moccasin with warm down-filled socks. The moccasins are worn with the snowshoes; the skier carries his pair while traveling. Moccasins alone are slippery because the leather soles freeze and provide little traction. They are difficult to hike in, but comfortable around camp. For winter camping, moccasins are probably warmest. Light moccasins around camp are also ideal for the canoeist or backpacker — moccasins give those tired feet a break.

BOOT CARE

Your boots will last for many seasons if you take the time to care for them.

To help keep the leather of new boots supple, apply some leather oil as soon as you get them home. Too much oil deteriorates the leather; too little oil causes it to crack. Once in a while, depending on the climate, boots have to be re-oiled. Some new boots come with a recommendation for a sealer for waterproofing. Most waterproofing solutions are made of silicone and function best if a few sparing coats are applied rather than one heavy coat.

As much as possible, keep leather boots dry. If they do get wet, apply more oil to prevent cracking. If you wear the boots in the wet, change your socks as they get wet. This will ensure a slow drying time. Allow a full day for boots to dry. Placing them in the hot sun or close to a fire shrinks and splits the leather.

In cold weather, moisture trapped in the leather can freeze and result in splits, so while winter camping, it is equally important to keep boots dry. Besides, wet boots mean wet feet, and wet feet are not fun.

While hiking, a blister may develop. As you feel it form, stop before it becomes more serious and place adhesive tape over the tender spot. If you continue hiking, and ignore your feet's warning, you will develop a raw sore that will hinder further hiking. It does not pay to be a martyr.

While hiking, it is pure pleasure to rinse those tired feet in a cool mountain stream. Clean feet seem to go an extra mile or so. (While enjoying the refreshing stream, keep your soap out of the water. Give the wilderness ecology a break.)

USED BOOTS

Old boots have some trade-in value at many sporting-goods stores. If you look around you may come across a good saving on a used pair. If they are a quality boot with reasonable wear (about one season), they will cost only a shade less than the original price. But, remember, if they don't fit, they are no bargain. If they do fit, they are already broken in and ready to go and are a bargain.

The Pack 7

Shopping for a new pack is fun. The stores are filled with packs in a variety of colors, materials, shapes, styles, and prices. Each pack has its own personality. Some things it does well, others not. First consider your style of camping and what you need from a pack. For wilderness camping, there are two choices in the type of pack: the rucksack and the packsack. There are also several other specialty packs, designed for skiing, day hiking, and canoe portaging.

THE HISTORIC RUCKSACK

For as long as people have been camping, the rucksack has been their main carrier. I have taken an old rucksack on many different camping trips. My brother gave it to me after it had been broken in. It was a large canvas sack with numerous side pockets for quick access to snacks, dry socks, and mosquito repellent. The leather arm-straps were wide but, unfortunately, not padded. The straps were designed to spread the weight across the shoulders. The entire pack was well constructed. It was made of sturdy canvas, tough leather, and reinforced buckles. The top flap was over-sized, so that my sleeping bag and shelter fly could fit underneath.

Rucksacks are available in lightweight nylon. Some packs also have a metal frame made from tubular aluminum which enables the entire pack to ride slightly higher on the back and makes a heavier load easier to carry. A frame also prevents the pack from lying flat against the back, allowing cool air to circulate and preventing a wet sweat spot from forming. A bellybuckle is another helpful feature. It holds the pack close to the back, improving balance. Some rucksacks taper slightly towards the top. Most rucksacks weigh approximately 30 ounces.

The rucksack's low-slung weight is its main advantage. A hiker with a rucksack will have a lower center of gravity than a hiker with a packframe, which makes balancing easier over rough ground, or when climbing hills, skiing, or portaging. The rucksack also allows free movement of the arms, essential for skiing, climbing, or portaging a canoe, and is easy to put on and pull off.

Another advantage is that rucksacks are less expensive than comparable backpacks. With a frame, a large rucksack can cost as little as $17. Better-quality sacks (such as made by Woods) are in the $30 range for the sack alone.

The major drawback of the rucksack is that it has a small load capacity. Compared to a packframe, the volume and the carrying weight of a rucksack are considerably less. When loaded, the shoulder straps pull back and the hiker must compensate by leaning forward. If you are taking a rucksack on a long trip, plan your gear very carefully.

THE BACKPACK: TECHNOLOGY CONTRIBUTES

The backpack is new to the camping scene. It has been mainly developed in North America using new materials and design, and, although efficient, it has some drawbacks.

A backpack, including both the frame and pack, weighs approximately 60 ounces. The frames are usually made of aluminum, the more expensive of magnesium. The aluminum frame weighs about 36 ounces; the magnesium frame is lighter but just as strong. These frames are curved to fit the shape of the back. The cross-braces must curve outward to prevent them from resting against the back. Because the frames do not flex, they carry the load more efficiently. Shoulder straps are padded, but some packs have soft padding which is deceptive — it may feel more comfortable in the store, but in the field it may not. When the pack is fully loaded, the soft padding flexes, and the force of the pack digs into your shoulders. A firmer padding spreads the load more evenly across the shoulders.

Most packs are made of heavy nylon. They vary in size, but most are approximately 8 inches deep, 16 inches wide, and 21 inches high. Some are divided into several sub-compartments for easy access. The pockets are usually nylon-zippered. Frames are available in many sizes — try them all on to find the packframe that fits you best.

Mini-rucksacks can be stuffed full with little restriction on movement. They are ideal for day hikes or climbs.

Taymor and World Famous are two Eastern manufactures that import packframes in a wide range of sizes and prices. A pack and frame can cost as little as $20. Since backpacks are difficult to repair, it is wise to pay a little more and get something more substantial. American-made backpacks are better made, but you pay more for them. A complete frame and pack can cost between $70 and $120. Some popular brands are: Camp Trails, Alpine Design, Sierra Designs, Gerry, Kelty, REI, Browning, and Mountain Master.

The backpack's big advantage is that it can carry so much. The inside of the pack is roomy; almost anything can be strapped to the frame. Because the frame places the load high on the shoulders and close to the back, the need for the body to lean forward, as required in packing the rucksack, is reduced. The walk is more upright. The bellybuckle places some of the load on the waist, holding the weight close to the lower back, increasing stability, and reducing backward pull from the load.

The major problem with the packsack is that it creates a high center of gravity. I once watched a young couple climb a steep mountain pass burdened with large backpacks. As they climbed, the packs appeared ready to summersault over their heads. The high center of gravity also made their balance awkward. Several times they stumbled because of the unnatural placement of the weight center. Also, the high frame makes it impossible to carry a canoe overhead. On our portages, Joanne carries our packframe and I the canoe pack and canoe.

The frame is a nuisance in the tent. If you stand it up anywhere, its feet will tear into the tent floor. Moving it in and out of the tent is a bother, since inevitably the feet catch in the mosquito netting. Although the zippered pockets keep their contents from falling out, zippers snag too frequently, especially, it seems, when someone is in a rush. When you use a backpack, take along spare pins; occasionally the zippers break. A loaded pack is also fairly awkward to pull on and off without help.

THE CANOE PACK

Oh, how I love it! It is huge. I stuff everything into it —the perfect pack for carrying big loads for short distances. However, because it is one big sack, it needs to be unpacked and repacked at each

Take your time when rolling up tents and sleeping bags in order to press out all the air, and so reduce bulk.

campsite. Also, it is not suitable for backpacking since it pulls the shoulders back.

Mine is made from heavy canvas and has sturdy leather straps. This winter I plan to add some padding to those straps.

The tumpline is a wide headband attached to the back of the pack, and I find it uncomfortable while walking because it strains my neck. I do use it if I am standing and want to rest my shoulders — I pull with my neck. The tumpline is also handy as a handle when I want to move the pack.

THE DAY PACK

These mini-rucksacks fold into themselves to form a small package. Popped out, they are big enough to carry a sizeable picnic for two, plus an extra sweater. Stuffed full, these packs do not restrict movement. They are ideal for day hikes or climbs.

THE FANNY PACK

These packs fit around the waist like a belt. They do not restrict any shoulder movement and are perfect for skiers or climbers. They do not hold a great deal, but do have room for a couple of chocolate bars, a pair of sunglasses, a can of juice, and an extra pair of mitts.

PACKING

The secret to successful packing is to travel light. The more you camp, the less you will find you need. It is difficult for beginners to think light.

Fill the bottom of your pack with light, bulky items such as sleeping bags and things that you will not need during the day. Pack heavier equipment and food in the middle or upper portion of the pack. Clothing will pack best if it is rolled rather than folded. The loaded pack should be balanced, so that when standing there is neither a pull forward nor backward. The straps must be adjusted so that the load does not pull out from the shoulders.

Know where each item is. If you have not developed a system, load your gear, unpack it, then repack it. It will help you remember.

Once, when packing food for a group before heading out on a two-week trip one of the members offered to help, and I unintentionally offended him by refusing it. I knew if we developed two systems, neither of us would know where things were.

Do not become too organized. One camper had a little cloth sack for almost everything — one was a toilet kit, another a tool kit, another contained a deck of cards, and so on. His gear was organized all right, but with so many sacks and pockets, looking for things became a chore because each sack had to be opened until the right item was found.

After a day or two, you will discover a place for everything and will want everything in its place.

MAKE-YOUR-OWN PACKS

Packs and pack frames are becoming more expensive each year. To help trim costs, you may want to make your own packsack or even packboard. Neither is difficult to make.

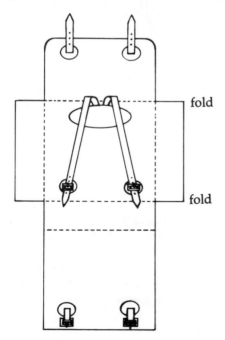

fold

fold

Packsack

This packsack is easy to make and you can decide how big you want it. Use either a light or heavy nylon or canvas. Rather than buckles, simply sew on string ties. Adjust the shoulder straps so that it sags low on your back. Depending on its size, it is ideal for afternoon walks, day hikes, or even overnight camping trips.

Packboard

Years ago, in Boy Scouts, we made these solid packboards and used them to carry a full load. We had fewer problems than boys with straight rucksacks. (Those were the days before backpacks.)

Use any wood, but select a strong, quality grade. A top-grade spruce is both strong and light; birch and maple are also good. Cherry is more expensive but has a beautiful grain.

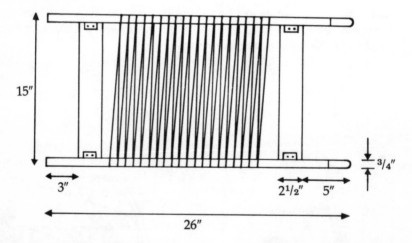

To make a packboard:

1. Cut two strips 26" long from 3"×1" (actually 2½"+¾") stock.
2. Round the top corners of the strips but leave the bottoms square.
3. Cut two crosspieces from 3"×1" stock, 15" long.
4. With a chisel or coping saw, cut out two channels for each crosspiece. The top of the upper crosspiece should be 5" from the top of the side. The bottom of the lower crosspiece should be 3" from the bottom.
5. Place the crosspieces into their channels.

6. Screw L-brackets in each corner securely and glue crosspieces tightly into channels. L-brackets are available at most hardware stores.
7. The completed frame will be 15″ wide, 26″ high, and 2¹/₂″ deep. From these measurements, you can design a frame proportionately of any size.
8. Along each edge of the upright pieces, file small curving grooves 1″ apart. Use a rat-tail file.
9. Lace nylon cord completely around the frame so that the cord lies in each groove. The cord will give the frame strength without adding much weight. The cord will also keep the carrier's back comfortable and cool.

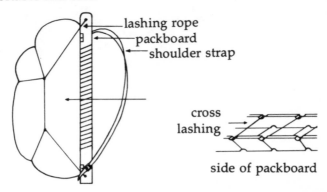

lashing rope
packboard
shoulder strap

cross
lashing

side of packboard

10. Mount the shoulder straps from around the top crosspiece of the frame at its center. Pass the straps through to be secured on the outside of the side pieces at the bottom with a buckle. These straps should be at least 2″ wide at the top and no more than 1″ wide where they meet the armpits. (If they are too wide at the armpits, they will irritate the skin.) Punch holes in the straps for adjustment. Although it does not appear as neat, the smooth side of the leather should be inside so that it will be easier to slide into and out of the frame. (You may prefer nylon straps with padding. These straps can be purchased at your sporting goods store.)
11. To pack, lay a large ground sheet over the frame. Place the load on the frame and bring the corners up so that it folds into one large bundle. Lash the bundle onto the frame. Packing is simple, but you cannot get at your pack unless you re-lash.

Shelter 8

Once, when camping in the southwestern United States, I discovered the pleasure of dropping off to sleep while watching the stars. Since then, in certain seasons and in favorable weather, I have occasionally been able to sleep outside without an enclosure of canvas. Unfortunately, most wilderness camping is in regions where the onslaught of insects is halted only by rain or cold, and shelter from the elements is necessary to receive that all-important rest.

Portable shelters have been with us for a long time. Long before the introduction of cloth, early people created shelters from wooden poles and animal skins. This simple design is still used during winter hunting trips by the Cree Indians in northern Ontario and Quebec.

With the development of cloth, tents became the permanent dwellings. Just as the Cree, the modern Arab nomad still uses a tent design that has passed the test of time.

The early people created shelters that best suited them. The wilderness camper is faced with the same need. He must consider type of construction, ease of erection, geography of the site, and availability of resources. The modern camper, however, has an advantage over the ancients: modern technology. It has increased the selection of materials, designs, shapes, and sizes. The selection, in fact, is so vast that many novice buyers become confused and purchase unsuitable or inadequate tents.

Before buying a tent, stop and think. Ask yourself where you plan to go, and what the campsite will be like. The shelter needs will be different if you plan to hike to the side of a rocky, windy mountain than if you plan to paddle through dense bush country. After considering the nature of your expedition to the wild, ask salesmen and experienced campers about tents.

Some of the cheaper models are imported by Taymor and World Famous and they are adequate for most camping needs. Quality tents are much more expensive. If you plan to do a lot of camping, these tents are a good investment. Manufacturers of quality tents are: Woods, Eureka, Thermos, and Ridgeline. Don't be surprised to see price stickers of $200 to $300. If you don't really know what you want, rent one for a weekend.

Read the rest of this chapter to familiarize yourself with types, designs, and materials. Armed with this information, you can make the right selection, and within your budget. Or perhaps, like me, you will decide to make your own tent. (See Chapter 9.)

TENT DESIGNS

For simplicity, tent designs can be divided into two types: family and pack tents.

Family tents are large enough to accommodate families or small groups. They are made from heavy canvas; some varieties are mounted on a trailer. Since they are not meant to be carried any great distance, their weight is not considered important. They are self-supporting, often by extensive use of poles and guy ropes. Some varieties are: wall tents, which are popular summer homes for Canadian Indians; umbrella tents, which are quick to erect; cottage tents, which are spacious and available with rooms; and, the infamous tent trailer, which travels anywhere the car can travel. None of these tents are suitable for the camper who wishes to strike off into the wild. They are too bulky and heavy to carry any distance and often are difficult to erect.

Pack tents are the only right type for the wilderness camper. The wilderness can only be seen from the side of a highway; to experience it, the camper must move himself and his gear into it. Because a pack tent must be carried, weight and rolled size are important considerations. Pack tents are seldom designed to sleep more than three. If you are planning to travel with a family or small group, privacy can be difficult to achieve. Two small tents rather than one large one are easier to carry and offer slightly more privacy, and, especially in bush country, a large, level site is seldom available. If you're traveling with children, as I sometimes do, it is more restful to have them a few yards, rather than just inches, away. Besides, kids enjoy the responsibility of their own tent.

Pack tents come in as many varieties as family tents and each one possesses special characteristics for particular camping needs. A bush camper, like myself, may prefer a tent that is stretched and secured by rope hung from trees, with the floor staked into the ground. For a backpacker, lightness and compactness are critical considerations, far more important than erected size. A mountain climber will consider both light weight and bulk but may need a tent that is totally self-supporting and windproof. Imagine erecting a tent on the side of a mountain without trees or soil in a thirty-five-mile per hour gale! The perfect tent for you, may be the worst for someone else.

THE TARP SHELTER

This simple shelter is an economical way to enter the world of wilderness camping. A simple sheet of material (plastic, nylon, or canvas) is cut between 9'×9' to 14'×14'. Reinforced grommets or ties are fixed to the corners and sides so that it can be slung between two trees or over a canoe, branch, or rope. More than once I have slept through some heavy rains warm and dry, tucked under plastic. Such a shelter is cheap, easy to set up, and compact to carry. On a hot day it offers shade and on a cool night it will keep the dew off your sleeping bag. I always carry one and use it as an extra fly. For sleeping, it is handy for weekend trips in areas with few bugs. (Take along fifty feet of rope.)

THE TUBE TENT

The tube tent is a cheap, disposable tent usually about nine feet long with an eight-foot circumference. The two-man model has a larger circumference (about twelve feet). These tents are plastic, so be sure to buy one made of at least four mil. They are simple to erect. All that is required is one rope strung through its length; it is then allowed to hang. A ground sheet is not necessary. If you are careful not to tear it or poke holes in it, you can get a lot of use for your $5.00. Be careful not to seal the ends; it will stop ventilation. (Remember, air cannot pass through plastic.) You may wish to buy a light-colored tent; you'll be less likely to trip over it at night.

Unfortunately, these little shelters are so cheap sloppy campers leave them behind when they pack out. The wind eventually blows the plastic into shreds, leaving an unsightly blot on the landscape. If you pack it in, pack it out.

FOREST TENTS

Forest or bush tents are designed for areas with lots of trees. A canoe tripper does not carry his equipment on his shoulders all day. Since he carries his gear only over portages, he can have a little extra weight in the form of a large tent, which can provide some extra comfort.

Forest tents have floors made from sturdy material and are more roomy than a backpacker's tent and a high roof creates more internal space. Poles with guy ropes or a center pole may be the major support. Or the tent may be designed to be slung from nearby trees or over a suspended rope. My forest tent is a simple pyramid design: it is quick to erect, sheds water well, is fairly roomy, and is sturdy against strong winds. It is my perfect tent. Complete plans are included in Appendix I, along with some other ideas on bush tents.

BACKPACKERS' TENTS

A smaller and lighter forest tent can be used as a backpacker's tent. Again weight and bulk are the key factors. The famous pup tent is a fine example of a popular backpacker's tent. If your hiking involves climbing steep mountain passes, weight is your major concern. Yet, on the other hand, if you normally hike along rolling trails, you may be interested in a little comfort with extra space. Frankly, I find some of these hikers' tents a little too cramped. Some are as difficult to get into and out of as a sleeping bag with a jammed zipper.

ALPINE TENTS

Alpine tents are for the mountain climber. His campsite is a rocky slope, exposed to cold and wind. To resist the wind, these tents have low roofs, and often an outside fly is provided to offer some extra insulation. Some are almost an inner and outer tent. Because of the lack of soil, no stakes can be used. The tent must be completely

Our homemade tent can be staked and slung up quickly and easily.

self-supporting with a complicated arrangement of poles. To minimize weight, poles are made of exotic materials. Some of the more expensive models have a small vestibule primarily for cooking. Naturally, a *small* stove must be used. Alpine tents are expensive and complicated. It would be difficult to make your own Alpine tent entirely from scratch, but you could cut costs by buying a kit.

TENT MATERIALS

Next to design, the material of your tent is the most important consideration. Basically, there are three types of materials available: nylon, canvas, and Egyptian cotton. Each has its strengths and weaknesses. Most pack-tent manufacturers have opted for nylon primarily to reduce costs. One of the reasons why I made my own tent was because there were so few made of Egyptian cotton. I feel that its advantages outweigh its weaknesses. But, as I have said, there is no perfect tent for everyone.

Nylon
Nylon is the cheapest and strongest. It is also light and rolls up without bulk. Cheaper nylon tents use nylon with a coarse weave which leaks and tears easily. Rip-stop nylon is best. It should be used on all tents — it is designed to stop tearing along its weave in case of a small hole.

Nylon has several drawbacks. Nylon tents tend to leak, especially after they have been used a season or two. The material pulls across the stitching leaving tiny holes. Since the fibres do not expand when wet like wet cotton, water can come in. Spraying or brushing the seams with a silicone waterproofer will rectify the problem for a short time, but this treatment must be repeated.

The other serious problem with nylon tents is that they do not breathe. As you sleep, moisture is released from your body in your breath and in body prespiration. The amount of water vapor released depends on the size and the number of occupants. The average person releases about a pint of water every eight hours. In the morning, the first person to rattle the walls of the tent triggers a morning shower.

Tent manufacturers take great pains to alleviate this problem. One solution is to sew ventilating windows into the walls and ceiling of the tent to equalize the relative humidity inside and out. This is fine if the outside air is of a reasonable temperature. But just try it in winter.

Another solution is found only on more expensive nylon tents. They are two tents: an inner tent made of a light blend of nylon and cotton which breathes, and an outer rainfly made of a plastic-coated nylon. The outer layer will keep the rain off, prevent leaks, and insulate the tent. It allows the canvas to warm up to above the dew point and moist air passes through without condensing.

One final word about nylon — you must be very careful around fires. A tiny spark will melt a hole the size of a quarter and an open flame, such as from a knocked-over gas stove, can turn the entire tent into a fireball. Nylon tents are more flammable than canvas tents.

Canvas
Canvas suitable for tent making comes in a variety of basic grades. There are several systems for grading canvas. Lighter canvas is graded by weight-per-square-yard, for example, 10 — ten ounces per square yard. Heavier canvas is given a grade or number, for example, 100. Obviously, heavier material is stronger. It is best suited for large, stationary family tents or winter tents. For winter camping, you get slightly more insulation from the heavier canvas. A fly also increases insulation.

For most purposes, the ten-ounce is strong enough and is easier to sew than the heavier canvas. It is also cheaper.

A main advantage of canvas is its ability to breathe. As moisture collects on the ceiling of the tent, canvas absorbs the moisture through to the outside air, and little or no water collects on the inside. There is no necessity for elaborate ventilating windows and complicated flies.

A canvas tent is also waterproof. As the fibers become wet, they expand and prevent water from seeping inside. The water then runs off. You must, however, be careful not to touch or to allow equipment to touch the tent ceiling. The inside pressure may break the water tension and cause seepage. Sometimes, after several seasons, canvas may lose its waterproof quality, but a light waterproofing treatment will restore it.

Canvas has two disadvantages: First, if not cared for properly, it will rot or mildew and the material will disintegrate. (Care must be given throughout the entire life of the tent. It must be stored clean and dry to ensure a long life). Second, it is fairly heavy. A ten-ounce canvas tent may not be overweight by most standards, but if you plan to backpack in the Rockies every ounce counts.

Egyptian Cotton (European Sailcloth)

Egyptian cotton or sailcloth is a finely woven canvas (about 200 threads per inch) that offers strength without excess weight. Originally, it came from the banks of the Nile River and was the major source of tent and sail material in the ancient world. Today, the Egyptian cotton plant is grown throughout the world; in North America, mainly in the southeastern United States. Its weight varies, but a six-ounce grade is advisable for tents. Besides being light and strong, it breathes very well. Most higher quality tents are made of Egyptian cotton.

Its major disadvantage is cost. It is more expensive than conventional canvas or nylon.

If you plan to make your own tent, you will find that Egyptian cotton is much easier to sew than nylon. Like canvas, cotton must be stored clean and dry; if not, mildew or rot can set in. If care is taken, you will be guaranteed many years of excellent service.

Prima cloth is sometimes available in the most expensive tents. It is polyester or nylon blended with cotton, having both the advantages and disadvantages of cotton and nylon. It seems like an excellent material, but commercial tents have a fly so apparently it does not have cotton's ability to breathe.

Choosing the material for the main body of your tent is an important consideration. Take your time. It would be tragic to make or buy a tent, then find it unsatisfactory because of cheap materials or inappropriate design.

A WET TENT

If you must pack a wet tent, dry it as soon as possible. When you get home hang it in your basement or garage. If on a canoe trip or hike, roll it out at lunch. Mildew and rot are the canvas tent's enemies, so take care.

66

MATERIALS

Characteristics	Nylon	Canvas 10 oz.	14 oz.	Egyptian Cotton Blended
approx. weight per sq. yd.	2 oz.	10 oz.	14 oz.	3 oz.
strength	good	good	good	good (fair for large tents)
breathing ability	poor	good	good	excellent
waterproofing ability	poor	good	excellent	good
price	low	medium	high	medium
retail price (approx.) per sq. yd.	$2.80	$3.60	$4.50	$3.50

All the above prices are the approximate retail price for fully treated materials — mothproofing, waterproofing, and rotproofing. Prices may vary from store to store depending on the manufacturers' treatment procedures.

Compare the total weights and costs of a forest-sized tent made exclusively of each of the three materials.

Sixteen yards of material for a tent shell of 7' x 9'

	Weight	Approx. Cost
Nylon	2 lbs	$44.80
Canvas, 10 oz.	10 lbs	$57.60
14 oz.	14 lbs	$72.00
Egyptian Cotton	3 lbs	$56.00

The completed tent weight and costs including the floor, ropes, and poles:

	Approx. Weight	Approx. Cost
Nylon	4 lbs	$54.00
Canvas, 10 oz.	12 lbs	$67.00
14 oz.	17 lbs	$82.00
Egyptian Cotton	5 lbs	$66.00

This homemade tent was sewn in a few evenings and cost was under $70.

TENT PEGS

The old wooden stakes are gradually disappearing, mainly because they split too easily. Steel stakes are sturdy but heavy and a surface rust soon develops which makes them dirty to handle. Unless you plan to drive them in during the spring and remove them in the fall, you may as well forget it. Aluminum pegs are compact, as they fit inside one another, but it is my experience that they bend easily and, once bent, develop a weak spot and bend even more easily.

Plastic pegs in bright colors are the most practical. They are strong, durable, and can be easily seen; hence, they are less likely to be left behind.

Occasionally, you may come across wire pins that are looped on one end and pointed on the other — they are only suitable in soil clear of rocks as they are designed to be pressed into the soil by hand.

WATERPROOFING

There is no such thing as a completely waterproof tent, but you can, and some day may have to, improve your tent's ability to repel water. New tents are pre-treated at the factory but after a couple of seasons you may have to reproof them. It's a simple task and will only take an hour or so. Do it on a sunny day. Waterproofing solutions come in paint-on or spray-on cans. The aerosol is more convenient but more expensive, and, since aerosols are potentially dangerous to the ecology, I avoid them.

Set up your tent and brush or spray on the silicone, and allow to dry. A light coat will do the job. The liquid in the solution evaporates leaving the silicone to help resist moisture. Naturally, the silicone will add a little weight, but not enough to worry about.

Some do-it-yourselfers make their own solution from melted wax and turpentine. Unfortunately, the turp will evaporate and leave the wax behind creating a major fire hazard. There have been several reports of people getting severely burned in such tents, and I strongly advise against do-it-yourself waterproofing.

Do-It-Yourself Tent Making 9

Most tents sold by commercial manufacturers are designed to fit the needs of the majority of buyers. After you develop your own style of camping, you begin to see weaknesses and strengths in the various designs. Your perfect tent should combine several features to meet your special needs. Your dream tent may be a combination of a special design, a specific material, and a unique method of support that cannot be bought in the marketplace.

By making your own tent, you will get exactly what you want, with quality construction, and at a considerable reduction in cost. And, there is a definite inner satisfaction one gets when sitting outside a self-made tent, surrounded by nature's own handiwork.

When I was in the market for a tent, I looked for one that was easy to erect, lightweight, and made of breathable Egyptian cotton. I do most of my camping in forest country via a canoe. Plenty of trees are easily accessible and so a tent that can be slung without poles is convenient. When trees are not available, the tent must adapt to a pole. After careful planning, Joanne and I set to work, and had soon made a small, comfortable tent for two. If you think that you would like to try, pull out a sharp pencil and paper and get started.

HOW TO START

First, read the previous chapter on shelter. Understand the types of materials and tent designs. Think of the way you camp and how that effects your needs. If family camping is your interest and you do most of it from a car, a large spacious tent designed to be self-supporting would seem the most logical choice. If you backpack, ski,

71

or snowshoe, you may prefer a small tent with less comfort space, and the tent may use poles staked to the ground. A mountaineer wants his tent to be as low as possible to reduce interference from strong winds, and because he may be setting up the tent on sheer rock, supporting poles must spread the floor. Since a canoeist does not have to carry his tent all day, a little extra room may be preferred at the cost of a few ounces. Camping in bush country means the tent can be slung from surrounding trees and bushes.

With a basic idea of your needs, visit your local sporting goods stores. Ask to see their tent catalogs and examine their displays. Ask about materials and designs. (You may find they know less than you do.) Take a pencil and paper and jot down notes and sketch details that interest you. These trips cost you nothing, but can teach you a lot, and when you have seen the prices of the latest tents, you will be convinced you can make your own.

Keep looking and sketching until you have collected a number of possible designs. Select your specific preferences and combine your various ideas into a composite of your perfect tent.

DESIGNING THE PERFECT TENT

Below are some guidelines and suggestions that will be helpful. You may wish to study the sketches of simple homemade tents included in Appendix II or even the complete plans included in Appendix I.

Floor Space

FAMILY TENTS

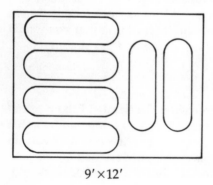
9'×12'

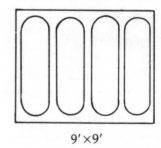
9'×9'

FOREST TENTS

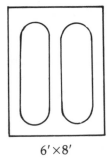 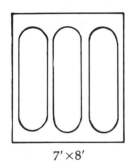

6'×8'   7'×8'

MOUNTAIN OR BACKPACK TENTS

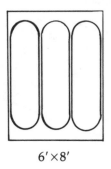 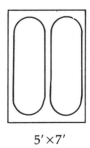 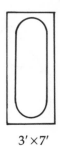

6'×8'   5'×7'   3'×7'

After considering floor space, examine the angle at which walls rise from the floor. As you can see, the sharper the angle, the less space.

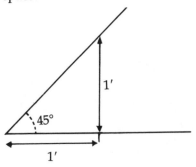 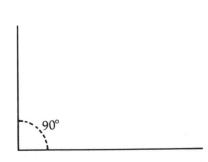

Tent Supports

a) Self-Supporting: *Hangs on poles*
Family: Cottage Tent   Backpack: Pup Tent

Hangs on a frame
Family: Umbrella Tent   Mountaineer: Pup Tent

b) Slung: *Hangs from exterior supports*, e.g. trees.

HANGS ON POLES

Family: Cottage Tent   Backpack: Pup Tent

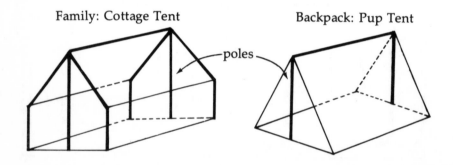

HANGS ON A FRAME

Family: Umbrella Tent

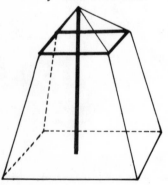

Mountaineer: Pup Tent

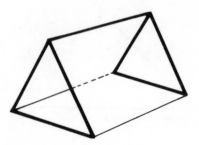

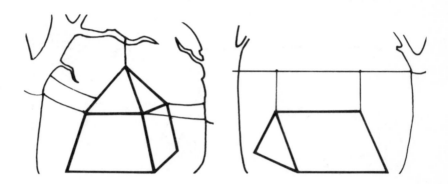

Pole-supporting

If you have decided to use poles, here are three methods of supporting your tent poles.

1) *Reinforced Ceiling*

   This method is best suited for tents with a peak in the center of the tent.

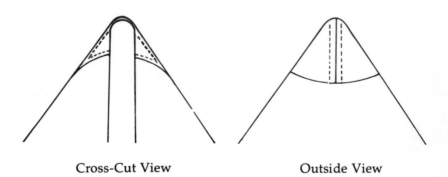

Cross-Cut View   Outside View

2) *Looped Rope*

A rope has been sewn into the tent roof. The pole is inserted through the rope.

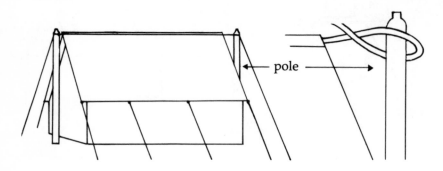

3) *Draped Method*

A third horizontal pole is used inside the tent. The upright poles are supported by guy ropes.

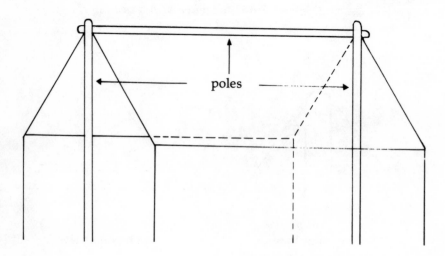

If you feel that rope-securing is the best method, here are three different methods for securing both the sides and the peak of the tent.

SUPPORTING BY ROPES

1) *Sewn Rope*
   Here, the rope or webbing is actually sewn onto a seam, because the material is not as strong as the seam. Webbing is much easier to sew than round rope. If the webbing is reasonably light, your sewing machine will be able to sew it without difficulty.

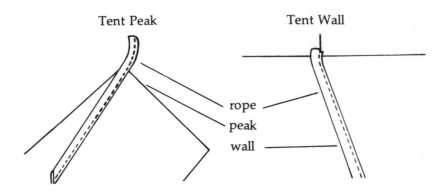

2) *Grommets*
   Grommets, two rings snapped together, can be bought at a hardware store. On a tent, they can be used at a peak or a wall.

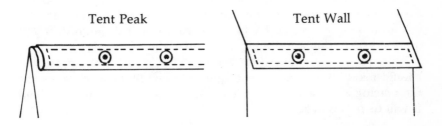

Corners can be folded for more strength, as seen below:

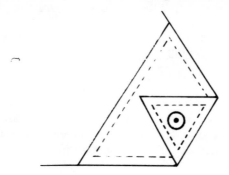

3) *Loops*
   Metal loops with one side flat can be used like grommets.

Floors

You can choose from a variety of materials. Canvas is water resistant, but there are two problems with a canvas floor: One, it gets dirty fast and is difficult to clean as the dirt works into the weave and, two, it allows moisture to seep up through the weave from the ground.

A plastic or rubberized floor usually will not allow moisture to enter but often has a slippery, cold feel. The strongest plastic or rubber floor has a nylon web reinforcing the back. The stronger the floor, the more expensive the material. Before buying any material, ask for a scrap piece and try to shove your finger through it. If you are successful, buy a more expensive material.

With plastic or rubberized floors, there is one precaution you should take; while drying or airing out your tent, never leave the floor facing a hot sun for long. The sun will dry out the material and it will turn to powder!

You may also wish to purchase some plastic for tarpaulins or ground sheets. Remember that anything less than ten mil will be like using sandwich wrap.

Screens

Nylon screens can be purchased at the same place as canvas. They are a must for camping in any area with insects, that is, camping anywhere in the world where the temperature is above freezing. Winter tents or ice-fishing huts obviously do not need screens. They should not use plastic floors either, as in the cold plastic will become brittle and tear.

Peg Loops

Peg loops are made from nylon or cotton webbing. Some people like to make their own by taking strips of leftover material and folding it into a loop.

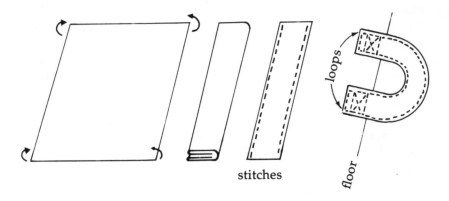

stitches

loops

floor

Zippers and Ties

Zippers can be sewn into doors and even windows. They are especially handy on family tents. Because of their weight, string ties of cotton or nylon are sometimes preferred on pack tents. Ties can be bought or made from scrap material in the same way as peg loops.

Another neat trick is to use Velcro. It is a tape about one-inch wide, with a coarse strip sewn on one flap and a softer side sewn on the other flap. The two strips stick when pressed together, but can be pulled apart easily. Velcro is designed to retain its stickiness. It can be bought at most fabric stores.

Ropes
For securing ends or peaks, ropes can be used. Other than the standard hemp and flax or polyester ropes, you may choose a flat webbing of cotton or nylon, which are reasonably priced and easier to sew than standard round rope.

Poles
For their weight, aluminum poles are the strongest. Generally, they are the best for family-type tents. Wooden poles are cheap but difficult to pack. Special lightweight poles made of complex metals will interest the mountain climber but are harder to find as well as being more expensive.

Threads
The wrong thread can destroy an otherwise excellent project. The purpose of the thread is to join pieces of material in a specific design. If the thread is not strong enough, the material will pull away under stress. Besides strength, the thread must also prevent water from leaking through the holes made by the needle and also prevent the material from stretching. A pure polyester thread is strong enough but does not prevent water from leaking through. A cotton thread stops the leaks since when it is wet the cotton expands to seal the needle holes. Cotton when new is also strong enough, but over the years it weakens. There are two other types of thread.

There is a thread available made of a polyester core, wrapped in cotton. The polyester provides longlasting strength, and the cotton plugs the holes when water runs on the seam. Even if the cotton decays, some of it will be left in the needle holes to keep the inside dry.

Some people complain that on their particular sewing machines cotton unravels while sewing. If this happens to you, two threads, one polyester and one cotton, can be threaded through a large needle. A straight polyester is all that is necessary on the bobbin.

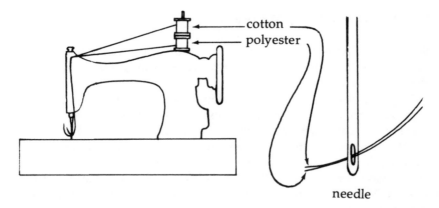

cotton

polyester

needle

THE LAYOUT

Now that you have a fair idea of your tent, calculate all the seam lengths. Appendix III includes three different methods of calculation. Next, make a list of each tent panel and its measurements. Add to the measurements, at least ³/₄ to 1 inch for seam allowance. Appendix I lists all of the pieces of the tent that Joanne and I made. You can use it as an example of how to list all of the panels.

For example:

Front side panel — two pieces right and left.

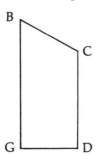

GD=36"
CD=60"
BC=43.26"
BG=80.625"

WHERE TO FIND THE MATERIAL

Some of the necessary materials can be ordered from a sewing or fabric store. Buy the combination polyester and cotton thread and the Velcro here also.

The best place to get canvas, nylon, screens, flooring, poles, and rope is from a custom canvas shop. These places make custom awnings, tarpaulins for boats and trailers, and repair tents. Prices are usually wholesale. Often, the men who work in these shops know canvas and love new ideas. They can be helpful if approached in a polite way. Look in the Yellow Pages under *Canvas*. If you live in a town with more than one such place, visit several and compare prices and advice.

After you have listed the measurements of all of the panels, find your material. Do not buy it immediately, but find out where you can get the material in the optimum width. It may come in 36, 42, or even 54-inch widths. Calculate the width with the least waste. Remember the seam allowance; at least $3/4$ to 1 inch is necessary around each piece. Be sure to measure the material. Sometimes a 36-inch width is actually only 35 inches. With only 35 inches plus seam allowance, the result is a piece of material 33 inches wide.

To save costs, use double pieces as much as possible. With proper spacing, you can save a lot. The back of the tent shown here is made of two pieces. These pieces are the same size but reversed. To save, cut the material like this:

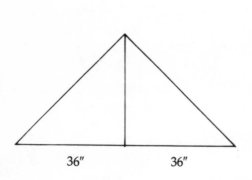

36"   36"

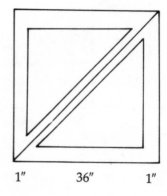

1"   36"   1"

Two precautions must be observed when calculating the material.
1) Some pieces will have to be cut into smaller sections and sewn together. Always have your seams joining the pieces running down the walls of the tent.

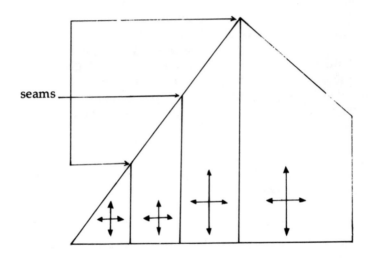

2) All materials, whether nylon, canvas, or Egyptian cotton, have a grain or flow of weaving called the *nap*. The nap of the material must be laid so that each adjoining section has the nap running in the same directions.

If it does not, the material will stretch into peculiar shapes; water will not run straight off; and the material will weaken and tear easily.

Now figure exactly how much material you need and the required width, then purchase your material.

CUTTING: ONLY ONCE!

Once you have bought your material, you have "put your money where your mouth is." It is now time to put your ideas and calculations to work.

Cutting can be easy and accurate when you know exactly what you want. On canvas and Egyptian cotton, a pencil marks easily and can be erased. Be sure to use a steel square at each corner; it ensures that the corners meet correctly when sewn. Do not trust the accuracy of the textile manufacturers; they do not need to be as accurate as you, and their corners are often slightly crooked.

At times, you will need to make a long, straight line. Fold the material from point to point. The crease left will give a straight accurate line. When handling long pieces, a friend is helpful.

The golden rule for cutting is "Always measure twice, and cut once!" Remember to add the seam allowance; it should be in your notes.

Once cut, the material can be rolled and labelled. Whether you like to cut, then sew, then cut some more, or cut all the pieces and then sew is not significant. What is important is to take your time and work in an orderly way.

SEWING: QUITE SIMPLE

Sewing is easy — as long as you can sew a straight stitch. Remember to use the combination thread (polyester and cotton) to save headaches later on.

There is one seam that has some advantages and is easy to sew. Called the *single-fold seam*, it is strong, neat and clean. The procedure is as follows:

1. Place the two pieces with their outside faces together.
2. Stitch down three-quarters of an inch from the edge.
3. Fold the top piece over so that the stitching is covered.
4. Now stitch one-quarter of an inch in on the right of the seam.

The stitch looks clean because only one stitch shows. It is easy because it does not require the skill to place two stitches together and keep them straight. It is strong because it is done twice.

When sewing that last seam, a friend can help to pass the material through the machine. In most cases, you will have to roll the right side of the material.

SINGLE-FOLD SEAM

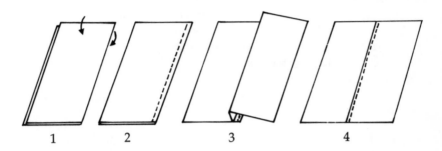

1 2 3 4

Make sure all reinforcing pieces are sewn before main pieces It is extremely difficult to sew them in after. When sewing peaks sew the short lines together first.

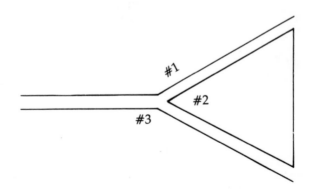

Sew #2 to #1
Then sew full length along
#3 from #1 to the end of #2.

When sewing the floor on to the tent, use the longest stitch available, especially if the floor material is plastic or rubber. If the stitching is too close, the floor may perforate, tearing at the needle holes. Stitch some extra pieces first to check for strength.

The floor should be sewn after the main tent body. Turn the tent inside out and sew the floor on upside down. When you have sewn twice around, pull the tent back. We made the mistake of sewing the floor from the outside. The finished tent had the seam outside and water lay on the seam and seeped into the tent. We ripped it out and sewed it again, as shown above.

Finish the tent by adding peg loops and tie strings. You are now ready to go!

Tools of the Kitchen 10

At home, when it is my turn to wash dishes, I am constantly amazed at the number and variety of kitchen tools "necessary" to produce the simplest of meals. Of course, when it is my turn to cook, I never notice. But when camping only the basic essentials can be taken along. Since you cannot take everything, what you take must do everything. In fact, to cook a simple meal in the wilds, you need very little.

THE MESS KIT

Without question, the best cooking kit is a set of lightweight pots which stack into one another. All the various-sized pots, plates, and cups form a neat bundle which is the size of the largest pot. These nesting kits are useful for all types of camping.

There are several varieties on the market with varying price ranges to fit your budget. The more expensive kits are easier to cook with. They dissipate heat better; the handles fit better and they resist dents better than economy kits. Look for these names: Mirro, Smilie, and Sigg. Prices vary from $8 for the cheapest 16-piece kit to $30 for a good-quality kit.

Since I often take groups out on camping trips, I find I can add or subtract the number and size of pots and plates to fit the group.

The major problem with camp cookware is heat resistance. For the sake of lightness, pots are made of thin aluminum which does not spread heat evenly. It is very, very easy to burn food. To help heat spread more evenly, I leave the black carbon (from the fire) on the pots. After a few meals, the carbon thickens and helps reduce scorching. Some campers recommend soaping pots before use; covering the outside bottoms of the cookware with liquid soap also helps in clean up. However, I have found that, unless you thoroughly clean the pots, the black gets all over you and everything else. I leave the black on until I get home, when I can tackle it with all the conveniences of home.

With groups of four to eight people, I take the following: one 8-qt. pot for use as a waterbucket, wash pail, or stewpot; one 4-qt. pot, primarily for cooking rice, mashed potatoes, or porridge; one 2-qt. pot for soup, meat, or mixing pudding and pancake batter, or cool drinks; one 2-qt. coffee pot for coffee, tea, or soup; and two skillets.

My skillets are aluminum and I must admit they make frying difficult. Careful heat control is a must, so if you have aluminum skillets, pack extra patience as well. The ideal is a solid cast iron pan; it spreads and holds the heat, but who needs all that extra weight? If you can get your hands on a couple of steel skillets that come with the kit, the extra weight would pay off in reduced black-cornered pancakes.

If you buy a nesting kit, check that the wire handles lock in the upright position. I have one pot that does not lock properly, and, unless I am careful, I'm sure to douse the fire with my lunch.

Plastic has improved the quality of camp plates and cups. I began camping with aluminum plates and mugs. During each meal, the hot food made the plate or cup too hot to hold and a short, two-second wait resulted in a meal too cold to enjoy. Unbreakable plastic has changed all that.

A homemade cotton sack helps keep all your kitchen equipment together and keeps the black on the pots and off the rest of your gear. A few minutes at a sewing machine with some scrap material will produce a washable duffle sack. If you are a little on the lazy side, a green garbage bag is almost as good.

A SCROUNGER'S KIT

If you are just starting to buy camping gear and your budget is low, you may be interested in the Scrounger's Kit. Here's how to make one: collect coffee tins of sizes varying from one to three lbs. (To get a

This size pot can be used for cooking, washing, or dousing the campfire.

pail-sized can, ask at a restaurant.) Punch two holes, and add a wire handle. A set of pliers can be used to lift the pots when hot.

UTENSILS

A knife, fork, and spoon that interlock are convenient for packing. The only necessary utensils are a spatula for frying and a large spoon. Make sure the handles are long — fires are hot!

FOIL

A heavy-duty grade of tin or aluminum foil is useful: used as a pot lid, it will keep ashes out of food (it can be re-used); it can be wrapped around pot or frying pan handles to serve as insulation. Foil is also indispensable in baking. Once on an overnight hike, each camper folded his meat, onions, carrots, and potatoes in foil and cooked his own. Some of them cooked the food together with the meat in the center, others cooked each item separately. That meal was the highlight of their wilderness adventure.

The main problem with foil is the waste. To protect the land, pack out all leftover foil.

A GRILL

On most trips, I do not bother to take a grill, which is often dirty and bulky. I build the fire so that it forms a solid log-cabin arrangement — the pots rest on the burning wood and on the fireplace rocks. If you do buy a grill, buy one that folds flat and stands with its four legs pressed into the ground. Otherwise it can fall over.

On a trip last summer, a friend brought along a small lightweight backpacker's grill. Made of a light metal, it measured about 15 inches by 4 inches and weighed only 4 ounces. It came with a small carrying case which kept the black off the other equipment. I really liked it and feel it well worth the $7.00 it cost. You do, however, need stones or large logs to rest it on.

90

A messkit is handy for all types of wilderness camping. Kits are available in a variety of sizes, prices, and qualities—but they must be lightweight.

REFLECTOR OVEN

Some campers believe a small, folding reflector oven is a must for any trip into the wilds. At the end of each day they set it up to bake bannock buns while they carry on cooking supper. By the time supper is ready, the buns are ready. I would rather do without the weight at the cost of hot buns, but it is up to you to decide.

POLYTUBES

These tubes have a screw cap on one end and are open at the other. Any soft staple can be pushed into the tube; the bottom is folded and held with a plastic clip. When you want the stuffing, unscrew the cap and squeeze the bottom. If you squeeze the top, you will probably find its contents on your lap. These tubes are convenient for jam, peanut butter, H.P. Sauce, Cheez Whiz, or any other delicacy.

DISHWASHING

Unfortunately, every meal eventually means a pile of dirty dishes and sticky pots. Fortunately, the job is limited to the number of pots and plates you brought with you. You need a large bar of non-detergent soap, a copper or nylon scouring pad, and a dish rag. Hot water helps cut the grease; heat water in the large pot and use it as a basin. A hot-water rinse follows the soapy wash. We leave dish towels at home. After a day in the wilds, damp towels seem to pick dirt off virtually everything. It is ridiculous to wipe dry, clean plates and pots with a dirt-and-germ-ridden towel. Instead, fan dishes in the air and lay them in the sun to dry for ten minutes. Do not dump the dirty water into clean lakes or streams. Pour the water onto ground that is deep enough to absorb the waste and decompose it. Use only biodegradable soap.

STOVES

With the ever increasing numbers of campers, our natural firewood supply is becoming scarcer and scarcer, but in most areas where I

92

camp, people are seldom seen and the few campers that do travel through consume a nominal amount of dead wood. Up in the Rockies, however, I once came across large areas where the hiker traffic had seriously depleted the naturally low wood supply. In these areas or in areas of high forest fire risk, a stove is essential. A small camping stove is a blessing on extremely hot days when cooking over an open fire would be torturous. A stove is also convenient on rainy days.

Most outdoor stores have a broad selection of small, light, single-burner stoves. Check that the stove in its folded state, along with fuel, is compact. Find out how long the fuel will last. A light, compact stove that needs several bulky cans of gas is no saving. Also, consider its safety and ease of operation.

One of the oldest fuels for burners is kerosene. It is safe and easy to light. Kerosene, however, emits a smelly smoke. Kerosene is sometimes hard to find.

Sterno stoves were one of the first designed for wilderness hikers. Often referred to as "canned heat," the fuel comes as a jelly in a small can. The fuel is alcohol-based and produces low heat, so you can count on a long cooking time. It is compact, safe, and the fuel is easily obtainable.

A single burner stove will cost around three dollars and a double burner will cost nearly five dollars.

The most popular fuel among lightweight campers today is butane. Available at most sporting stores, it is easy to light, but does not burn with much heat. In cold temperatures, it takes forever to boil water. I remember once finishing a day's travel through a steady rain. Our group was ready for hot chocolate to restore some warmth to our cold bodies. One of the fellows set up his butane stove to heat one medium-sized pot of water. The rest of us set out to collect firewood in the rain-drenched forest. It took us a long time to find the right materials to light a fire, and by the time we had the fire going, a half-hour had passed. Only then did the water on the butane stove start to boil. Needless to say, I am not overly impressed with butane burners. A simple folding stove costs about ten dollars. Each cartridge lasts for about four hours, costs $1.50 each.

Propane burners are also popular. They produce good heat but not as much heat as white gas; the fuel cylinders are heavy but last up to four hours.

Another advantage of propane is that the cylinders can be refilled. A simple stove will cost around $15, about $2 per cylinder.

White-gas burners are the most efficient and cleanest of all backpacking stoves. They are also the most volatile, so follow directions carefully and keep the flame-opening clean. White gas is used by all of the big-name manufacturers, such as Primus, Optimus, and Sula. The better models of these powerful little stoves boil a quart of water in three minutes. A stove with a tank capacity of one pint burns for about two hours. A small stove costs about $20; the bigger burners about $35.

These stoves can be tricky to light especially in cold weather. If it resists lighting, prime it first by placing a little fuel down its vaporizing tube.

Before buying, shop around first to get a full picture of what is available. Ask questions, and try lighting the stove a few times at the store. You'll soon get some idea of what you like.

Food   11

When you are in the wilds, meals take on a new importance. Days spent in fresh air and exercise stimulate the appetite. If rest is the foundation, meals are the cornerstone for a successful camping adventure. Many of your most memorable times will be centered around planning, cooking, and eating. Good eating on the trail starts with thoughtful planning at home.

PLANNING

First, consider the four basic camping and personal needs: nutrition, flavor, ease of preparation, carrying weight, and bulk.

Nutrition
If you are eating well-balanced meals before embarking on your wilderness adventure, you need not become overly concerned about vitamins and minerals. Even a trip as long as two or three weeks will not upset your vitamin and mineral balance, provided you try for a balance. The major change will be energy consumption, increased by outdoor exercise. Generally, a man traveling outdoors — canoeing, hiking, skiing, or snowshoeing — will burn about 3,500 calories a day. In cold weather, the energy required to keep warm could boost his calorie need to over 4,500. But, everyone has different energy needs, so one formula cannot be applied to everyone. Exactly how much food to take will depend on your metabolism and the amount of exercise taken.

Sometimes I meet people who see a wilderness trip as a fantastic opportunity to lose weight. The problem is that a pound of body weight represents over 3,000 calories. If a person cuts his calorie intake by half, a one-week trip will result in a small weight loss of three to four pounds. If the cost of this loss is a miserable trip, then the question is, is it worth it?

Your calories come from three sources. Carbohydrates are quickly digested and absorbed and provide quick energy for a short time. Starch, found in rice, peas, corn, potatoes, and bread, is one type of carbohydrate; another is sugar, found in fruits and candy. The fats found in meats, cooking oils, and butter are another energy source. Excess fat is stored in the body and can be broken up into heat very quickly. I was once with some elderly Eskimo men who had some raw fat from a caribou. To these experts, the fat was a candy treat, its ability to produce heat meant survival in their frozen land. The last energy-producing food is protein. Because of the complicated molecular structure of protein, it consumes energy in order to break itself down into energy. However, the energy that it produces has a longer effect. Protein is also important for tissue-rebuilding, especially for tired muscles. Some protein sources are: liver, meat, eggs, milk, whole wheat grains, and fish. Include all three types of energy sources when buying supplies for your trip.

Flavor

Outdoor life revitalizes the senses of taste and smell. The taste of food improves and enjoyment increases. In the wilderness you may develop new tastes, and foods that were unattractive to you at home may become tempting. Take food that you enjoy even if it means carrying a little extra weight.

Ease of Preparation

Your menu-planning must also take spoilage and ease of preparation into account. All food that will spoil without refrigeration must be left at home. Cooking time of more than thirty minutes will make meal preparation painfully slow. Be flexible — you can use different items at various meals. Perhaps on a cold morning, for example, the mug of soup planned for the evening meal would be more tempting. There are limits though — I still do not find porridge for supper appetizing.

Weight and Bulk

Whatever you decide to eat, you have to carry. You are limited to the volume of your packs and how much weight you can carry. Water in food creates the largest percentage of the weight — dehydrated and freeze-dried foods greatly lighten the load. Seeds, nuts, and grains take up little space for their weight and have high-energy yields. You soon develop certain favorite foods for which you become willing to accept the extra weight by reducing somewhere else. Plan for about 1¹/₂ lbs. of dry food per person per day. In the event of poor weather, it is wise to include food for an extra lay-over day.

SOME FOOD IDEAS

Meat

A hard, spiced salami or summer sausage keeps well without refrigeration, but it is a little heavy. It can be eaten from the hand, thrown into stews, lightly fried, or made into sandwiches. Any delicatessen has a selection, but do not make the mistake of pre-slicing it. Slicing infects the meat with bacteria and causes early spoilage. Other smoked meats (such as bacon) will also keep. When you are buying bacon, check that it is not artifically smoke-flavored. (Smoking preserves the bacon; artificial smoking does not.) The fat on the bacon can be used for other cooking. Bacon will become moldy unless washed in a solution of vinegar and salt and wrapped in cheesecloth. Since the meat releases moisture, its covering must breathe. Keep it out of the sun. On your first evening out, you may wish to have your favorite steak, chops, or ribs deliciously barbecued — After all, it will be your last chance for a while.

Fats: Lard and Margarine

Margarine stuffs neatly into polytubes or plastic bags, but goes stale after a week; lard keeps longer. For long trips, butter in a can is a safe bet.

Cheese

Unsliced cheese wrapped in plastic keeps and carries well. If mold forms, just scrape it off; it will not spoil the rest of the cheese. To help reduce mold, paint a thick coat of baking soda and water over the cheese and wash it off before using.

Milk
Powdered milk is the obvious substitute for fresh milk.

Bread
Heavy, dark European bread such as black rye and pumpernickel keeps well for a few days. It is filling and does not crush as easily as spongy white bread. On the trail, bread-like buns, bannock, can be made: before leaving, mix 1 cup of all-purpose flour, 1 teaspoon of baking powder, and about 1 teaspoon of salt. The result is similar to pre-mixed biscuit mix. When you are ready for fresh bread add $1/3$ cup of water or milk. Pour it into a greased frying pan to a thickness of about 1 inch and cover. Cook slowly over very low heat for about 10 minutes. To make a crust on both sides, I sometimes cook it for about 7 minutes or until the edges brown, pull it away from the sides of the pan, and flip it into another greased pan to cook for five more minutes. To make buns on a reflector oven, place the oven near the fire and place small dabs of mixed dough on the shelf. When dinner is cooked, your buns should be golden brown and ready to eat.

Rice
You may prefer the quick-cooking converted rice but I like natural-grained rice. It is less bulky for its cooked results and less expensive.

Instant Foods
Instant mashed potatoes have improved over the last few years; quick-cook oatmeal is easy to make; and instant puddings and packaged soups are tasty and quick to prepare.

Snacks
One summer, I took trips out for a small camp in Haliburton, Ontario. Each day, we snacked on raisins. They are highly nutritious, produce quick energy, and help reduce irregularity. After the first couple of days, I was nicknamed "Raisin-head" but not because of facial wrinkles. Another trail snack is "gorp." Mix together any ratio of raisins, peanuts, cashews, almonds, dried prunes, jelly beans, candies, some sugar, pretzels, Shreddies, Cheerios, a sprinkle of salt, chocolate chips, dried fruit, or anything else that you think will taste good and keep well. Package it in small snack-sized plastic bags and keep it handy for quick energy.

Dehydrated Food

Dehydrated food is made by putting it into a vacuum and drawing the water out of the vacuum by heating. Powdered milk, instant potatoes, and instant coffee are examples. All are extremely useful on the trail.

Freeze-Dried Foods

In this case, the food is frozen very quickly at very low temperatures. It is then placed into a vacuum and heated. The moisture sublimates into the air: it changes from a solid to a gas without changing into a liquid. The food juices are left and only the water is removed. The process is expensive, but the result is very light. When cooking freeze-dried foods, the directions must be followed religiously or a steak will have the taste and consistency of cardboard. Because of the harsh processing, some people find freeze-dried food difficult to digest. One must also consider the damage the process must do to vitamin balance. Manufacturers of freeze-dried foods produce a large variety of vegetables, fruits, meats, and combined pre-cooked lunches. The pre-cooked meals, particularly, are full of heavy seasonings and synthetic chemicals. Some are tasty, such as the chili con carne, others are rather bland. Try a variety to see which ones you prefer. In spite of the processing damage, I use freeze-dried foods frequently on trips longer than a week. I supplement them with fresh fish, fresh salami, and the odd can of meat. The extra weight of these supplies adds variety to an otherwise 100 per cent freeze-dried diet.

Good brands are: Hardee Foods, Gumpert's Mountain House, and Stow-A-Way. On page 100 is a partial chart to give you an idea of what to expect when purchasing freeze-dried food.

Seasonings

Do not forget salt. Your body is constantly releasing salt in sweat and urine, and it has to be replaced. Most freeze-dried vegetables do not contain enough salt. H.P. sauce, carried in a polytube, helps activate the flavor of freeze-dried meats. Bouillion cubes and dried onions can be added to soups and stews or even used as a noon drink on a cold day. Why not toss soup mix and vegetables into a pot of rice, or spruce up instant potatoes by adding some cheese spread? Use your imagination — it's fun.

Freeze-Dried Foods

	Weight per Package	Unit Serving	Price
Complete Meals			
Chicken Stew	3.6 oz.	2.8 oz.	$2.65
Beef with Rice	4.8 oz.	2.8 oz.	2.45
Chili Con Carne	5.5 oz.	2.8 oz.	2.65
Rice and Chicken	4.8 oz.	2.8 oz.	2.00
Chicken Chop Suey	3.4 oz.	2.8 oz.	2.80
Franks and Beans	5.0 oz.	2.8 oz.	2.80
Shrimp Creole	3.8 oz.	2.8 oz.	2.70
Noodles and Meat Sauce	4.5 oz.	2.8 oz.	2.45
Potato Patty			
with Ground Beef	4.5 oz.	2.8 oz.	2.45
Meats			
Chicken—Diced	2.4 oz.	2	2.65
Pork Chops—Boneless	2.1 oz.	4 chops	4.50
Beef Patties	3.4 oz.	4 patties	3.65
Beef Steak	2.5 oz.	4 steaks	4.60
Vegetables			
Peas	1.8 oz.	3-4	1.30
Carrots	1.0 oz.	3-4	1.25
Green Beans	0.5 oz.	3-4	1.30
Corn	2.0 oz.	3-4	1.30
Fruit			
Apples	1.0 oz.	2	1.15
Apple Sauce	1.5 oz.	2	1.15
Peaches	1.0 oz.	2	1.25
Strawberries	1.0 oz.	2	1.35
Breakfast			
Plain Omelette	2.0 oz.	2	1.65
Cheese Omelette	2.4 oz.	2	1.80
Ham Omelette	2.4 oz.	2	1.85

PACKING FOOD

Your aim is to reduce the load to its lowest weight and smallest bulk and keep the whole thing organized. First, lay out the entire load on the floor. Eliminate all boxes by pouring single-meal portions into sandwich bags. The best bags are large enough to allow you to tie a small knot. (Fold-lock type bags will leak.) Before sealing the bag, stuff in the label corner and note on it any directions such as quantity of water required. If you are packaging instant pudding, add the required powdered milk, and note on the label how much water to add. As you seal the bag, squeeze out all excess air.

After all the items are repackaged, use larger bags to package each meal. For example, one supper may include one meat, a bag of instant potatoes, some freeze-dried corn, dry soup, and pudding. Place all breakfasts, lunches, and suppers into separate green garbage bags and place each meal bag into separate packs. When you need a meal, reach in and pull out a surprise.

Or, package all the meats together, vegetables together, desserts together, etc.; then pull out your choice of each. The method which you choose is not important; the convenience lies in the prepackaging of each item into meal units.

A MENU OUTLINE

Menus depend on each person's food habits. You will soon develop your own preferences; no one regime is the ultimate, but do experiment. Below is a suggested outline to help you work out your own menu. Change the combinations for variety.

Breakfast
- hot cereal — oatmeal, Red River, Cream of Wheat
- pancakes with honey, jam, or syrup
- freeze-dried eggs with cheese, ham, or mushrooms
- coffee or tea
- an orange-flavored drink (with vitamins)
- an instant-breakfast drink

Trail Snacks
- raisins
- chocolate

- cheese or salami
- gorp (*see page 98.*)
- fruit — orange, apple, or grapefruit

Lunch
- loaf of heavy bread
- bannock with canned meat, tuna, corned beef, honey, or jam
- freeze-dried lunches — chili con carne, stew, or shrimp creole
- Kraft Dinner (with added cheese)
- salami or summer sausage
- packaged corned beef (for the first day)

Supper
- dried soup
- meats — canned (ham or chicken)
  — freeze-dried (pork chops, steaks, ground beef, or chicken)
- starch — rice, instant potatoes
- vegetables — freeze-dried (peas, corn, green beans, onions)
- dessert — instant pudding
  — freeze-dried apple (excellent), peaches and strawberries (fair)
  — Inside-Outside Cake (*see page 103.*)

COOKING TIPS

Be organized. After a hectic first day, you will soon develop a simple system. Stick to it to avoid confusion and frustration.

Cooking in high altitudes takes longer; since the air is thinner, water will boil at a lower temperature than at sea level.

BOILING

Altitude in feet	Increase in cooking time
3,000	20 per cent
4,000	30 per cent
5,000	40 per cent
6,000	50 per cent
7,000	60 per cent
8,000	90 per cent
8,000 plus	a pressure cooker recommended

BAKING

Altitude in feet	Decrease in amount of baking powder
3,000	10 per cent
6,000	25 per cent
10,000	30 per cent

You may wish to eat a cold lunch to save time. Make bannock at breakfast, then have it for lunch with tuna, meat, honey, or jam. A sweet drink gives quick energy. I have had this lunch often, resting in a canoe while drifting with the wind.

My famous *Inside-Outside Cake* can be made for a special celebration: Soak your favorite dried or freeze-dried fruit, and, as it is soaking, make up a thick batter of bannock. Pack the batter into a grapefruit-sized ball and wrap it in foil. With your fingers, poke a hole in the batter and spoon in a healthy helping of fruit and a heaping tablespoon of brown sugar. Plug the hole. Completely cover the whole ball in foil, then cover in hot coals and ashes. Occasionally turn the ball. Bake for about 15-20 minutes. Enjoy.

Outguessing the Weather 12

No one is more vulnerable to changes in weather than the wilderness camper. Changes in temperature, wind, and air moisture dramatically change the wilderness environment and the camper can do nothing about them. Folklore has created a host of old wives tales for long-range forecasting — for example, the squirrel that saves an extra large pile of cones knows that the next winter will be long. Neither folklore nor modern science has come up with reliable long-range prediction methods. Science and technology have developed sophisticated short-range forecasting schemes but these resources are not available to the wilderness camper. Some campers take a pocket radio for the purpose of checking the weather. I prefer to leave it behind and rely on my own observations of natural weather indicators. Besides, radio forecasts are usually too far away to be accurate. With some practice, it is easy to develop a sense for weather. The skill will help you to decide on doubtful mornings whether to break camp and head on to the trail or to sit tight. By watching the sky and observing changes in temperature, wind direction, and even air pressure, you become aware of nature's constant changing moods. Rather than fight the elements, learn to camp in harmony with them and feel that you are a part of the wilderness.

FACTS ABOUT THE WEATHER

Different weather conditions depend on the changing relationships between temperature, pressure, wind, and air moisture. These variables affect the weather interdependently.

Air is heated by the sun; as it warms, it expands and becomes lighter. This light, warm air rises as heavier cold air moves in beneath it. This air movement is called "convection" and is the cause of local breezes. Wind is also created by the earth's rotation. Because the earth's surface moves faster at the equator than at latitude 60°, latitude has an influence on the prevailing winds.

As the sun warms the air and the surface of bodies of water, air scoops up molecules of water and clings to them as if they were particles. The warm air then rises, carrying the moisture upwards. As it leaves the warm surface, it begins to cool. Since the ability of air to carry water is dependent upon temperature, the cooler air has a problem holding on to the moisture. Clouds form when the air has reached a relative humidity of 100 per cent, that is, when the quantity of the water vapor held by the air is equal to the maximum quantity of moisture the air is capable of holding at that specific temperature. Once a cloud has developed, there is a potential for precipitation.

As the cloud is heated during a sunny day, it begins to rise and expand, and becomes loose and billowy. These single, fluffy clouds are called *cumulus* clouds.

Air movement can create a flat, continuous cloud-layer, covering the country like a blanket. This is called a *stratus* cloud.

Cumulus and *stratus* are the two basic cloud types that appear at various altitudes in infinite numbers of shapes.

Low Clouds (below 6,500 ft.)

Cumulus are fluffy clouds with flat bottoms. Because they need the upward movement of warm air, they often disappear at night. They are a sign of fair weather.

Fractocumulus are cumulus clouds that have been torn apart by high winds. They move quickly across the sky and usually by evening have dwindled, leaving a clear sky.

Stratocumulus clouds may give some light showers, but they do not contain very much moisture. Usually in the afternoon, they begin to break apart to provide a glorious sunset, then disappear leaving a clear, night sky.

Stratus clouds often give a light rain, very seldom a heavy rain. They appear as a flat, continuous layer.

Nimbostratus clouds are similar to stratus clouds but darker and denser. They appear as a gray, flat blanket lying low over the earth.

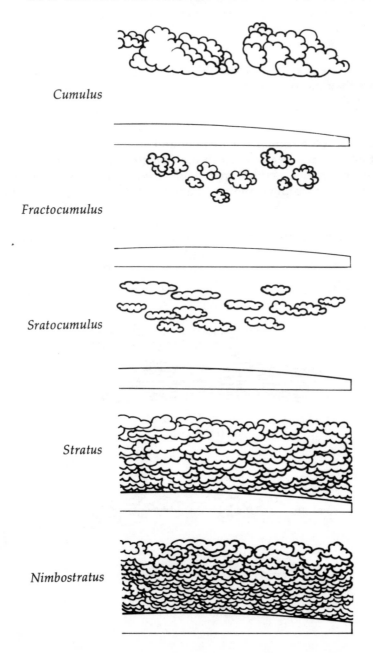

Cumulus

Fractocumulus

Sratocumulus

Stratus

Nimbostratus

107

Mid-Height Clouds (bottoms about 10,000 ft.)
At this altitude, the two basic cloud formations develop: cumulus and stratus.

Altostratus are gray, hazy clouds that give one that dull-day feeling. Usually they mean a steady rain is coming. They appear flat, with occasional streaks or spots.

Altocumulus are a sign of fair weather and appear after a storm or as the stratus clouds begin to break up. Sometimes they will begin to pile on top of one another and their bottoms will turn gray — a warning that a storm is coming in about eight hours.

MID-RANGE CLOUDS WITH THEIR BOTTOMS ABOUT 10,000
FEET

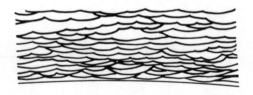

Altostratus

Altocumulus

High Clouds (bottoms about 20,000 ft.)

Cirrus clouds look like thin wisps and curls and are often called *mare's tails*. They are created by the warmth of the morning sun and disappear around noon.

Cirrostratus clouds form a thick gray layer above the cirrus wisps. If they begin to thicken, rain or snow is only a day or two away. These clouds form a hazy ring around the moon or sun.

Cirrocumulus are small clouds rippled by the wind into a wavy pattern. They are not thick enough to block much sunlight. They normally disappear by the afternoon. Like the friendly cumulus, the cirrocumulus is a sign of fair weather.

Cumulonimbus appear on hot, humid days. Piles of puffy cumulus build a pyramid cloud, flat on the bottom, and rising thousands of feet to a fluffy top. Sometimes the very top is windblown by the high-altitude winds: The bottom is gray or even black. This is the classic *thunderhead*, a sure sign of coming rain. If it is approaching, you are sitting in a warm front. Cooler air is pushing the cloud towards you. The warm air is rapidly being pushed upward as the cold is forced downward. This violent movement of air creates the huge pile of clouds, which, because of the changing temperature, are becoming desperate to release their moisture. Usually, you can see the rain pouring in blankets at the base. It's an exhilarating experience to watch one of these giants roll slowly towards you. In a few minutes the day darkens and the temperature drops. This cold air precedes the storm by about three miles, so you have about a minute to seek shelter or get your poncho out.

If there is lightning, you can count the seconds to determine how far away the storm is. One second between the sighting of the flash and the sound of the thunder equals approximately one mile.

The rain hits and passes as abruptly as it came. Pushing the cloud is cool, fresh air. After it leaves, the wilderness smells clean and fresh. The damp trees and rocks capture and reflect light, improving the contrasts and making the outdoors even more beautiful. It's a super time for photographers.

During a thunderstorm, take some safety precautions. As the thunder rolls closer, seek shelter and stay away from water and

HIGH CLOUDS WITH THEIR BOTTOMS ABOUT 20,000 FEET

Cirrus

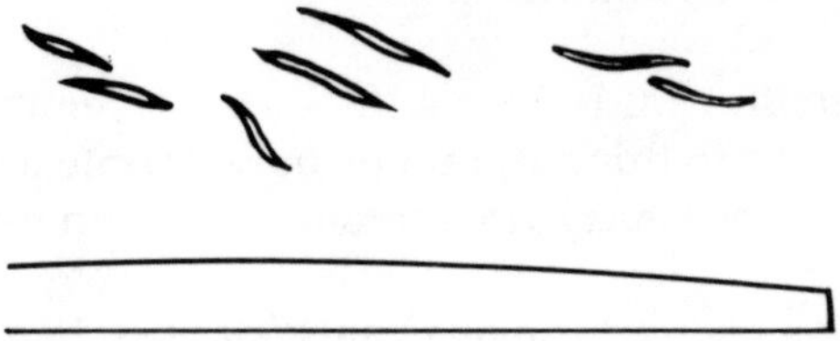

Cirrostratus

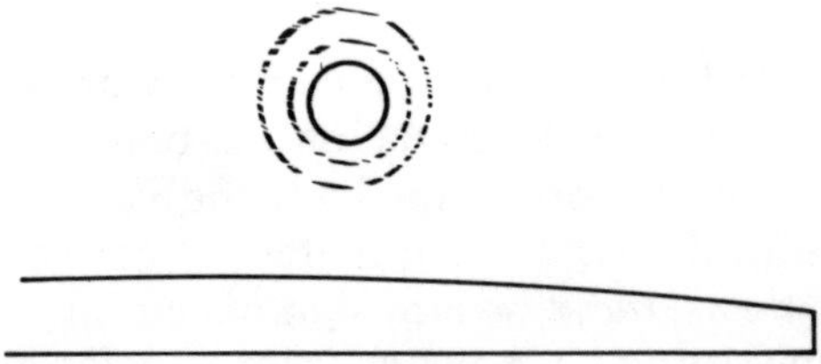

Cirrocumulus

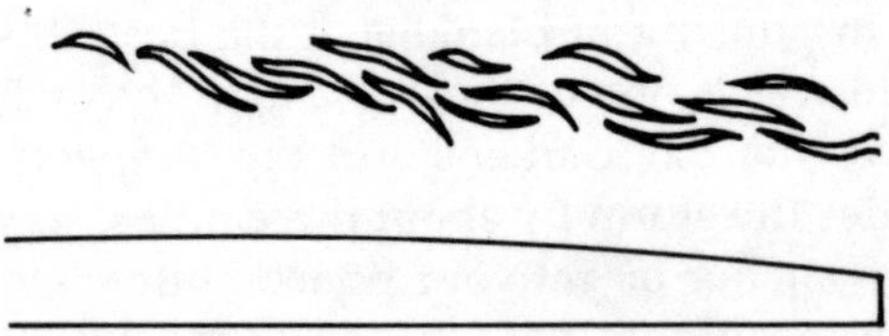

Cumulonimbus

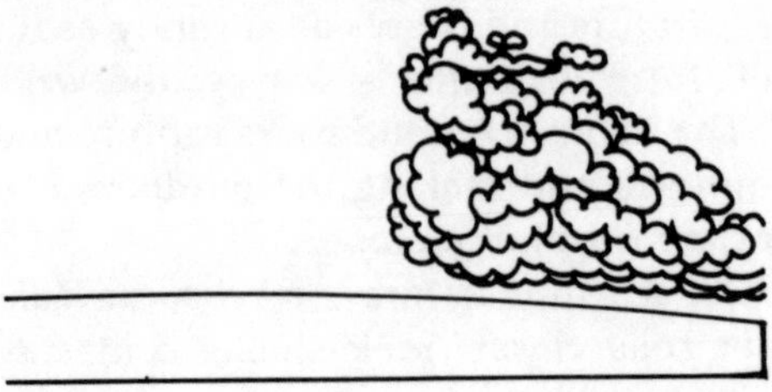

solitary trees. Hide under low trees, rock crevices, or overhanging banks. If you are trapped in open space, lie prone. Believe it or not, your chances of not getting hit by lightning are very good if you are not sheltered and are out in the open. The storm is exciting so enjoy it, but play it safe.

AIR PRESSURE

Air pressure, whether high or low, has an important role in influencing weather changes. Air moves from a high-pressure area to a low-pressure area. When you stop to think about it, it makes sense — like water flowing from a high point to a low. Since in a high-pressure area, air is moving away, steady fair weather will stay. The temperatures whether warm or cold, will vary little. In a low area, air movements are traveling in bringing unsteady temperatures, changing cloud formations, and a high chance of rain or snow. You may feel you need a barometer to measure air pressure, but there are several natural signs that can give a clue to changing pressures.

WILDERNESS WEATHER SIGNS

Ducks will fly high if the weather will be good, but low if rain is on its way. With coming rain, birds will sit closer to the tree trunk rather than out on the small branches. Your campfire smoke will rise straight for fair weather but it will hang low if rain is coming. With the rise in air humidity, hemp rope, canvas, and wooden-handled hatchets will tighten with the swelling of moisture. Curly hair will become even more unmanageable. Insect-eating birds feed less with poor weather coming.

With the changes in pressure and humidity, you may hear distant sounds more clearly. Smells from swamps and marshes will be stronger. If you have rheumatism, corns, or ulcers, you will be aware of weather changes.

111

MORE WEATHER SIGNS

Below are some weather signs. Remember them the next time you go out, whether for an afternoon walk or a three-week wilderness adventure.

Clearing
- Wind shifts to the west
- Clouds begin to rise to higher altitudes

Possible Temperature Drop
- Wind shift to north or northwest
- Clear nights and little breeze

Possible Temperature Rise
- South wind at night with cloud cover
- Clear day sky

Possible Rain or Snow
- Red sunrise
- An increase in the speed of a southerly wind with clouds from the west moving in
- Dark western sky
- Winds shifting counterclockwise
- Thickening cirrus clouds
- Cumulus clouds piling up in the afternoon
- Ring around the moon, a halo
- Dry at night, with no dew
- Temperature at night higher than usual

Fair Weather
- A gentle breeze from the west or southwest
- Dew in the morning
- Morning fog breaks within three hours of sunrise
- Cumulus clouds in an afternoon sky
- Clouds disappear between 3 and 5 p.m.
- A red sunset

Remember the poem:
Red sky in the morning, sailor take warning;
Red sky at night, sailor's delight.

Finding Your Way 13

Often, when traveling with a group of young campers, I've been asked, "Where are we?" with slight hints of worry in their voices. With a smile I reply, "Well I can't tell where we are but I know we are not lost." It is true. I take mental notes of outstanding landmarks such as a stream, or a rotting tree, and of the general direction we've been traveling in. Half the battle in keeping your sense of direction is observance; the battle is lost when you count on intuition.

Without an accurate guide, either a compass or landmarks, it is incredibly easy to become disoriented. A buddy of mine and I once hiked only a quarter of a mile through the bush to fish in a small lake. Since it was such a short distance, we didn't bother checking our compass on the way out. We headed south from the lake and came on a trail which we thought was heading south. It was the wierdest sensation to arrive back at the lake. If you don't believe it, blindfold yourself at the goal line of a football field. Try to walk straight for a hundred yards to the other goal. Soon you'll find yourself walking in the wrong direction. It seems as if the spinning of the earth tips the delicate balance organs in the inner ear. Direction by senses is a losing proposition.

The Compass

The simplest solution to the direction problem is a compass. You should never step into the wilderness without one; to do so is asking for trouble. A dependable compass should be one of your first purchases.

A compass is simply a magnetized needle that has the ability to pivot. The earth is covered with a magnetic field which causes the needle to swing, pointing to the north magnetic pole with one end and the south magnetic pole with the other.

Buy one with a sturdy, rugged case. The case should have a hole or loop so that you can tie it to your belt-loop or string it around your neck. Check its ability to withstand interference. Place a metal object near it and watch for any deflection of the needle. Any deflection with the object greater than two to three feet away is unacceptable. A luminous dial is handy, but I never travel in the bush at night anyway. Spend a dollar or two more and get a compass that is fluid-filled. Without the fluid, the needle oscillates with the slightest jiggle, and it is annoying to wait for it to stabilize. If you have the cash, you may want one with a sighting device.

I bought a medium-priced Silva for around $12. I like it because it is simple; it's easy to read, durable, and has a straight measuring edge in both inches and centimeters. (Useful for reading maps.) It also has a small magnifying glass that not only helps in seeing fine detail on maps but also can be used in a pinch to light a fire. Top-of-the-line compasses are the Sunnto KB-14 and the Silva 15T.

Using a Compass

My brother Rick and I broke camp early one morning and headed out into a thick fog. We paddled a mile or so down a bay in a large lake. When we reached the end of the bay, a wall of fog faced us. Somewhere, four miles away, was a tiny channel, among hundreds of others, marking our route.

Here's what to do:
- Place the compass on the map with the edge of the compass base along the desired line of travel. (In other words we aligned the base of the compass from our present location, a tiny unnamed bay, to our desired destination, a small channel.)

- Turn the dial of the compass until the needle points parallel with the angled line on the bottom of the map. Since the compass needle points to the magnetic pole, there exists a correction factor provided at the bottom of all topographical maps. This angle of declination can be important. With a 15° error, you can find yourself off course by 1/4 mile for every mile.

- Without changing the dial setting, turn the entire compass horizontally until the magnetic needle points to *North* on the dial. The direction of travel will now be pointing on the base of the compass.

Off we paddled, with the compass lying on the bottom of the canoe. By sterning, we held the magnetic needle pointing to the *North* on the dial and followed the direction pointing from the base.

Using a compass sounds complicated on paper. It really isn't when you've got a good compass in your hand and a map on your lap. Follow the directions that are enclosed with your new compass, and buy a map of your area. Go out and practice. It could save a life — your life.

AN EMERGENCY COMPASS

Take a small, thin piece of metal such as a needle or pin. Stroke it from eye to point with some silk or a magnet. Poke the needle through a couple of small pieces of bark and float it in some very still water, such as in a filled bowl. The needle will swing towards the north magnetic pole. If you rub it from point to eye, it will point south.

DIRECTION FROM A WATCH

I must confess I never wear a watch, least of all when I'm camping. I enjoy waking up when I have finished sleeping and not because it is

117

morning time, eating when I'm hungry and not because it is meal time; and stopping or continuing to hike according to how I feel, and not because it is or is not quitting time. I listen to my body's needs, not the mechanical instrument on my wrist. Experts claim a watch is necessary to know when to quit when the day is cloudy and you can't tell how much daylight is left. My body tells me it's tired; then I know there's not much light left. They claim that a watch can help you tell direction if you've lost your compass. Well, you need the sun and, with the sun, I can tell direction more accurately using the method below.

If you have a watch and you wish to tell direction, hold the watch so that the hour-hand faces the sun. A point halfway between the hour hand and the figure *twelve* will show south approximately. If it is before 6 p.m. use the smallest angle shown and after 6 p.m. use the largest.

DIRECTION FROM SHADOWS

This method will give an accurate direction towards true north, providing the sun is bright enough to cast a shadow.

Drive a short pole into the ground. To be certain that it is vertical, hold a weighted string beside it. Adjust the pole so that it is parallel to your homemade plumb-line.

Using the string, tie it to the base of the stake; pull tight; then draw a half-circle. Watch the shadow of the pole; mark where it becomes the shortest. At this point, the shadow will point due north.

DIRECTION FROM THE STARS

Most of us can easily find the Polaris star, but for review, it is included here. Find the Big Dipper, and note the two pointer stars on the outer edge. These stars point to the pole star, Polaris, which appears above the opening on the Big Dipper. The Polaris can be identified by its brilliance and its position as the end star on the handle of the Little Dipper. Facing that star, you will be within one degree of true north.

DIRECTION FROM NATURAL INDICATORS

It's wise to know the direction of the prevailing winds. In open country, you will observe that snow, sand drifts, etc., develop on the downwind side of wind-blocking objects. Wind-blown branches or fallen trees from the prevailing winds can also indicate direction. In eastern Canada and the United States, the tops of pines and hemlocks often bend eastward because of prevailing westerlies.

Some trees, such as pine, spruce, and other softwoods, tend to grow thicker on the south side. The bark of poplar trees is whitest on the south side, probably because of bleaching from the sun. Anthills will establish themselves on the warmer, south side of trees.

Moss grows more thickly on the south side of a tree that is open to the sun. The shady side provides more moisture. But be careful; some lichens can be easily mistaken for moss and they grow the same on both sides. All in all, nothing replaces a good compass and a topographical map.

The Wilderness Campsite 14

·After hiking all day in the warm sun, your body begins to relay messages. You begin to think of soaking swollen feet, sipping a cool drink, and letting sore shoulders rest. The campsite is your wilderness home; it's a place to relax and rest, feed a hungry stomach; and share your feelings of the day. It does not matter how you get there — hike, paddle, or ski — the campsite is special. To make your site comfortable, here are a few tips to keep in mind.

FINDING THE RIGHT SITE

A site must provide four basic needs: a level spot for the tent, cooking space, access to drinking water, and firewood (if you plan to cook with a fire). Camping parks supply these needs along with extras; the back country often does not. Deep in the bush a clearing for a tent may be a rarity, and, in arid country, water may be scarce. Early in the afternoon start to make mental notes of potential sites, and begin to reflect on your comfort needs besides the four basic ones mentioned above. If you want to fish, a site near a falls may bring a special treat for breakfast. If it's windy, a campsite sheltered by rocks or trees is desirable. If it is hot and sunny, shade adds a great deal of comfort. I often camp during the bug season; a breezy and open site provides considerable relief. To pitch camp in damp, swampy areas is to invite every insect for a free meal on your flesh.

One of the joys of wilderness camping is experiencing the natural wilds without the impact of man. Every year, with more and more campers trooping off into the wilds, it becomes increasingly impor-

121

tant to protect the environment. For us and our future generations to enjoy the wilderness, we must take responsibility now. If at all possible, choose a site that has been used before. Don't hack out a new one at the expense of living trees. Yet if the site looks over-used, travel on a bit farther to allow this site to grow back. Avoid camping on fragile plants and delicate wildflowers; stay out of mountain meadows. Camping there can inhibit growth for many years. Camp near trees where the soil is deeper.

Watch for dead trees that could blow down on top of you. I've seen the remains of a tent after a tree blew down following a storm, and, believe me, the tree came out better than the tent.

Check that the site is not a dried riverbed. A flash storm will prove to be beyond your tent's waterproofing.

I recall once camping near the edge of a river with a huge power dam downstream. In the evening, when the demand for electricity decreased, the penstocks were closed. Naturally, the water rose but at an alarming rate, and we were eighteen miles upstream. In the morning, the penstocks were opened for full power. So, if you're camping on a river, watch for dams, flash storms, and tides that could change the water level.

If you are camping in mountainous regions, watch for signs of potential rockslides.

If you are canoeing, good campsites are often found at portage sites. (The bush may be too thick along the banks.)

As I travel, I mark potential campsites on my topographical maps, especially beautiful sites beside waterfalls or with exceptional views, in case some other time I may get an opportunity to use these special sites.

SETTING UP CAMP

Once you have found your site, take a minute to pick up any bits of garbage left behind by previous campers. Unfortunately, some campers do leave reminders of their stay.

The first major decision is: where do I put the fire? The second, where do I put the tent in relation to the fire? Chapter 15 discusses

Once the tent is laid out, pull the corners tight, then peg them.

fireplace location and building. Set your tent site a safe distance from the fire. A tiny spark could easily melt a hole the size of a quarter in your tent roof.

My experience with groups from two to twelve has taught me that teamwork makes for a smooth-running camp. At first, novices are uncertain of what has to be done, but they soon catch on. Each member has his task: ideally, just as supper nears readiness, the tents should be up. Depending on the group, we may switch roles. When I travel with my wife, we tend to keep our favorite tasks.

Morning sun on the tent walls helps rouse the camp a little earlier; you may wish to position the tent with this in mind. Before unrolling the tent, clear the area of sharp rocks and twigs. Rather than hack out a live root, build up a little soil around it to prevent it poking through the tent floor. When pitching the tent, follow the directions that came with it. The manufacturer knows best how to set it up. If your tent requires that you stake down the four corners, make sure they are pulled tight. Once the tent is set up, adjust the tensions on the guy ropes so that the tent roof and walls are smooth. The guy ropes should stretch the tent with an even, balanced tension. If one corner is too taut, the tent will be deformed, stretching the seams.

With the tent up, unroll your sleeping bags and fluff the down. If the tent is on a bit of a slope, sleeping with your head highest helps avoid headaches. If you try sleeping across the slope, you'll find, in the morning, that everyone has rolled into the lowest wall and has formed a human stack.

If the tent is set up properly, rain should roll off it and away. Occasionally, because of a slight slope in the ground away from the tent, a rain trench may be necessary. It is best to avoid digging pits or trenches, but if it is necessary save the turf and put it back before you leave.

When the tent site has been selected, the fireplace located, and a wood pile formed, choose a small kitchen area up wind of the fire. With all the food and cooking utensils in one area, scrambling around the site is greatly reduced. People are drawn to the fire, and, if the food and cooking equipment are spread around, campers are forced to step over it. All too often things get stepped on. Or, almost as bad, the sand from their boots drops into water, pots, and food. It's unnerving when eating one's butterscotch pudding to suddenly grind on some sand.

TASK LIST

1. Clean up previous campers' waste.
2. Select fire location.
3. Set up tent.
4. Roll out sleeping bags.
5. Fetch water.
6. Collect firewood.
7. Build fireplace.
8. Set out food and cooking equipment for dinner.

THE WINTER CAMPSITE

Much the same principles apply to winter camping as to summer camping; but there are some differences. Winter camping demands that the pace be slower. More care must be taken in planning the clothing, food, and shelter. Nothing can be forgotten. When setting up the campsite, slow down all movements to avoid overheating. With warm winter clothes and hard work, your body perspires easily. Once damp, clothing loses much of its insulating properties and a chill can easily set in.

Set up your campsite away from potential snowslides. Read the section warning of slides in Chapter 17. Often snow will drift over rock crevices hiding a potential hazard. Before setting up camp, poke around the area with a pole to uncover any dangerous crevices.

One advantage of winter camping is that it is easy to make a level tent site. Even on a slope, you can dig into the snow to make a smooth level tent site. If the snow is soft, pack it with skis or snowshoes. Sometimes it is too loose and fluffy to pack. In this case scrape the area clear until you reach a firm base.

The tent should be located at an angle away or even across from prevailing winds. If it is facing into the wind, snow will blow into the tent. If the tent is facing directly out of the wind, snow will drift in front of the door. During a storm, it could easily bury you. Some protection from the wind can be provided by digging down into the snow or building up a wall around the tent. Leave a space about a foot wide between the snow and the tent wall.

Pegging the tent can be awkward in cold weather. If the snow is soft, make a snowball around the peg and bury it in the snow. (The hard-packed snow will hold the peg down.) Often the snow is shallow and the ground frozen solid. Trying to drive pegs into the ground is futile. The easiest way then is to peg with stones. If stones are not available, heat some snow until it turns into mush. Lay the peg on the ground and pack the mush around it. In a few minutes, the peg will be frozen solid, ready for its guy rope or floor loop. When you are ready to break camp, carefully chip the ice away from the peg.

Water is not hard to get in the winter, but melted snow is bland. You can improve its flavor with Tang or lemonade. The sugar gives fast energy which is soon used for body heat. Snow can be eaten for water, but since your body has to supply heat to melt it, eat it in small portions. Overeating snow causes chilling.

Often high altitudes and cold weather dull the appetite. Since your body needs extra calories to burn for heat, a poor appetite can be dangerous. So take along your favorite meals. Make certain you are eating an adequate amount. Eat your evening meal at least one hour before sleeping. With a full, undigested meal, the stomach requires extra circulation, otherwise used for body heat. A partially digested meal helps reduce the body chill that follows when you relax.

When winter camping nothing can beat a good down sleeping bag. Ventilate your tent during the night to allow fresh air to circulate. (More than one camper has had a tent heater going, consuming too much oxygen.)

In the morning, frost may have collected on the top side of your sleeping bag. To remove it, give the bag a good shake.

To make an igloo, pile some snow into a mound and pack it with snowshoes or skis. Tunnel into it as you did when you were a child and poke through a vent hole for circulation.

COMFORT TIPS

If the weather becomes unbearably hot, soak a blanket in water and drape it over the tent. It will cool your oven-like tent and may make sleeping easier.

If it gets cold, make this simple tent heater. Place a number of stones about the size of grapefruits in the fire. When they are very hot, put them under an inverted metal pail or large pot. (Be sure that the stones are resting on some wood and not melting the tent floor.)

If the tent is zipped up tight, there will be little air circulation. During a heavy rain, moisture from your breath will become trapped and condense on tent walls. By morning, everything in the tent will feel damp so let some air circulate.

PRECIOUS WATER

In most uninhabited lands, clean fresh water is plentiful. It is a pleasure to dip in and drink from icy mountain streams. Unfortunately, pollution is creeping into the wilderness and at times the purity of the water is questionable. It's claimed that water will purify itself in a lively bubbling stream in 30 feet of rocks and sand. Organic materials disappear, but harsher chemicals take much longer. If you are in doubt, play it safe: boil or treat water.

Boiling water, then cooling it, takes time, but it may be your wisest choice. Hold the boil for at least five minutes. Usually, if I suspect the water, I drink tea or a hot orange drink.

To treat water, use halozone tablets, which can be purchased from drugstores or camping stores (one tablet per pint of water). It leaves a chlorine taste, but the taste can be disguised with sugar and flavor crystals. It's not like a fresh stream, but it's better than getting sick.

In some areas, finding water may be a problem. High in the mountains you can usually find snow tucked in the shaded north side of ridges or cliffs. Remember that water will always flow downhill, so check valleys and gorges. Keep an eye peeled for moisture-loving vegetation. Willows, cedars, and cottonwoods like damp soil. If necessary, dig shallow wells at the base of these trees or at the outside bend in a dried river.

If you plan on carrying water, each person will need two quarts per day, if engaged in light activity; four or more if engaged in heavy activity. Water, if you have to carry it, becomes precious.

FIRST TIMERS

If you have never camped before or have never even set up a tent, go camp for a day — to a local park or even your backyard. Set up your tent and cook a meal. The experience will clue you into the jobs that need to be done. The practice will also give you confidence.

Sooner or later, even with careful planning, you will be knocked off schedule and will find yourself setting up in the blackest of nights. This may be a nerve-racking experience, if you are unsure of how to set up a campsite. Take your time and be organized. By morning you'll marvel at your surroundings and joke about walking into one another the night before. It's really nothing to be frightened of.

The Campfire   15

A campfire adds a certain romance to the wilderness experience. The hypnotic movement of colored flames, the fragrance of the rising smoke, and the hiss and crackle of burning wood are relaxing and fulfilling. But a fire has many uses. It can be used to cook, melt snow, or purify water. You can dry out and warm up by a fire. In an emergency, a fire can signal for help. It is unfortunate that many wilderness areas are becoming so heavily traveled that firewood has become scarce. In these areas, fires should only be made when absolutely necessary. For cooking, stoves should be carried in. All campfires and cooking fires must be kept small. Since natural wood-fuel takes so long to be replaced, avoid waste.

THE FIRE SITE

If a fire site has already been used, it is wise to reuse it. This will reduce the deleterious effect which your camping has on the environment. If there is no fire site, build a good fireplace and leave it clean so that future campers will use it.

The safest location is on bar rock; sandy or clay soil is next best. Dark, loamy soil containing decomposing organic material makes the poorest location. Take care: a smoldering ember can lie for a week, then break out and cause a forest fire.

Check overhead for dry, dead branches that could ignite. Break them down, or, better yet, move to another spot. The fire site should be protected from the wind — if not, heat cannot rise to the pots and heat them. Wind will also blow sparks and ashes over the ground, creating a serious fire hazard. If you are camping in the winter, snow on pine branches overhead may melt on the fire below. While cooking, you will not get a continuous drip; the grand finale comes when the whole snow pile slips off, plopping into your half-cooked meal.

If it is cold, build the fire so that you can sit between it and a large rock. In this way, the heat will reflect back off the rock and warm the spot where you are sitting.

Use your trowel to scrape away the brush, dead grass, and leaves. Clear the area of porous rocks. These contain moisture, and, as they heat up, water expands, often exploding the rock and sending forth tiny shrapnel-like pieces.

If your fire site must be on loamy soil dig a pit several inches down. Line the edge of the pit with stones or rocks, and fill in the cracks with dirt cleaned of organic material. Do it carefully and there will be no danger of an underground ember.

If there are rocks around, I usually build a U-shaped wall with the opening angled upwind. Sometimes the wind cooperates and keeps the smoke out of my eyes. This stone arrangement is perfect for a grill. The lightweight backpackers' grill is handy; it only weighs 4 ounces, measures about 5"×16", and costs around $7.

Often I cook without a grill by building a solid log cabin fire. I lay the pots directly on the half-burning sticks, and balance their edges on rocks. The pots partially smother the air circulation, slowing the burning rate and lowering the heat.

THE SECRETS OF SUCCESSFUL FIRE-LIGHTING

The rain was still pouring down at dawn. I was with a small group of young kids miles in the bush — with borrowed tents. The tents were faulty and everything was soaked. We were hungry and cold; and, needless to say, our morale was at an all-time low. All hope was placed on a steaming breakfast of hot porridge, but no fire, no porridge. We did, however, get our porridge. Always remember, even with the entire forest drenched, all materials to light a fire (except a match) are there. The secret of successful fire-lighting is to know what to look for, and to know a few tricks.

130

First, scrape away all organic material. Second, remember that a match cannot ignite anything larger than a match. Third, fine pine twigs make excellent tinder. Fourth, break up the tinder into a tight ball, then light.

An old scout-leader of mine put it in a nutshell: "A match will not ignite anything larger than a match."

Fuel that a single match can light is called *tinder*. Some campers use paper rather than look for tinder. But paper gets damp easily and when it burns leaves a large ash which smothers the budding flame. Some experts use dry weeds, but most weeds that I have used have been "punky," that is, too soft, and they don't burn with much heat.

On that rainy morning, gasoline would have been helpful. So I headed into the bush looking for something with gasoline-like properties. I was searching for two types of tinder. First, white birch with some loose bark. (Do not peel the bark off, rely on what is loose or lying on the ground.) Birchbark contains an oil substance that burns slowly with considerable heat, and, even though the bark may be damp, a match will ignite it.

Second, look for very fine needles and twigs on the branches of pine or spruce trees. They contain a dried resin which burns rapidly with high heat. On that wet morning, I crawled under the lower branches looking for the dead, dry lower branches and on the lee side of trees. Under some downed trees I found a large handful of dry needles and fine twigs.

The next step was to collect kindling, tiny pieces of wood about the thickness of a pencil. I collected a few handfuls and shaved off the wet bark. (Even dry bark does not burn very well.) The kindling was dead and the insides were dry. Green wood is still living and the moisture inside prevents it from burning well. Rotting wood often contains moisture and the more it has rotted, the fewer combustible elements are left. The best kindling breaks with a snap.

Next I collected a small armful of fuel. Again this was dead wood and its insides were dry, since it snapped when broken. All the pieces were no more than one inch in diameter, the thickness of a thumb. Soft woods, such as balsam, poplar, pine, cedar, and spruce, burn quickly and are most useful in getting a fire going. Hard woods, such as maple, ash, elm, and birch, burn more slowly, but give more coals and heat. Hence, they are ideal for cooking.

After breaking up the wood, I was ready to build the fire. Many books claim the best way is to make little teepees of ever larger sticks.

I follow these simple steps:
- Keep water handy for extinguishing

- Lay a base of one-inch sticks
- Crumple a ball of pine tinder or birchbark
- Light the tinder and slowly add pieces of kindling
- Add fuel
- Arrange coals for cooking

Allow the base of the fire to burn well before adding the next layer, and you will have few problems. If you add more fuel before the base has sufficient heat, chances are you will suffocate it, because this method allows the budding flame to receive plenty of air. If it needs more air, blow gently under the fire, not on top of it. If the fire does not catch after the second match, something is wrong; start over and avoid wasting more matches.

On wet days, I always place some pieces of fuel around the fire to dry. Like the kindling, I also shave off the wet bark to help it ignite. Once the fire is going, keep it small and under control. With practice, you will soon be rearranging coals as if you were turning burners up or down on a stove.

When you are finished with your fire site, burn up all of the half-burnt fuel. Leave a clean site. Soak your fireplace thoroughly. If you cannot put your bare hand into the soaked pit, it has not been soaked enough.

All the materials necessary to make a fire, except one, are readily available in most wilderness areas. The exception is the match. Because of this, I always carry extra packs wrapped in plastic and hidden in my pack. One is in the first-aid kit, another in my personal gear, and another in the food pack.

Some fire-lighters dream of mastering the old blow method. This friction method done well is an art, and it can be mastered with patience, hard work, and practice. It is something you may wish to try, but not appropriate for learning on the trail.

In the event that my matches fail (they never have), I sometimes carry a cheap, disposable butane lighter. Mine is rusty, but still works even when wet. Waterproof matches (made in Australia by Coghlan) are another alternative. They work very well. You may wish to make your own waterproof matches by dipping wooden strike-anywhere matches into barely melted paraffin wax. Before using, simply scrape off the wax on the match head.

Camping and Ecology   16

I have seen wilderness campers approaching a trip as if it were a campaign. Each day, they pack up before dawn and strike off as if it were a continuing rat race. For all that they see and experience, they might as well be hiking laps around a quarter-mile track. Their pleasure seems to come from a sense of achievement based on conquering as many miles as possible in rough conditions. But the wilds are full of subtle changes. Each new land formation brings a change in vegetation and of the creatures living in it. As you travel, take notice of the soil, the trees, the grasses, and the thousand tiny roles each item plays in building an ecological system. You will never learn all the names of the plants or insects, but names are not important. What is important is to see and feel a world not under the influence of mankind.

Consider taking a day or two off from the normal routine. When you find a special campsite with a spectacular waterfall or breathtaking mountain view, stay put for an extra day. Allow time to soak up the greatness of God's creation.

When the urge calls, take the trowel and paper to some spot where someone will not likely be walking. Dig a small pit about four to six inches deep. At this depth, the bacterial activity is high and the waste will decompose rapidly. Bury the paper as you fill in the pit, and cover it thoroughly. White paper is ecologically sound since it decays completely. Colored paper contains certain dyes that take longer to decay.

At a campsite, dig a small trench to a 6-inch depth at a known-to-all location. An ideal location is behind a downed tree about 1½ feet from the ground. I can never forget one beautiful latrine we made. We had found a white birch downed by lightning. The tree was secluded from camp but not too far away. Perched on the tree, we had a gorgeous view overlooking the river.

Keep the toilet paper wrapped in a plastic bag with the trowel. Paper is absolutely useless when it becomes wet. (When the paper and trowel are gone, you know someone is using the facilities.) Before leaving the campsite, fill in the pit and pack it down tightly.

You may be camping in rock areas where the lack of soil makes it impossible to dig a latrine. A hole can be made by rolling a large stone back and forth. Dig into the depression and, when you are finished, sprinkle back the dirt and replace the stone.

If you are camping in severe sub-zero temperature, be very careful to dry yourself thoroughly. Exposed and wet skin will freeze without feeling in seconds. When I worked in Frobisher Bay, N.W.T., there were a few reported cases of frostbite in some very embarassing locations.

You will also find that the cold air will force you to urinate more often.

In the cold, you may drink more than your usual amount of hot tea, coffee, or chocolate. All of these have ingredients that activate your urinary system. You may soon find yourself uncomfortable so keep an eye on how much you consume and adjust your consumption accordingly.

If you are washing in sub-zero temperature, wash small sections then pat dry immediately. Splashing water over your face in extreme temperatures will invite frostbite.

Help the rivers and lakes remain clean by washing yourself, your clothes, and the dishes from a pail. Use a biodegradable soap, then dump the soapy water on the ground. Choose a spot that will give the soil an opportunity to absorb the soap and water so that, in time, it will break down.

You should take the time to wash your clothes, especially the ones that you wear closest to your skin. Dry them on sunny rocks, bushes, or guy ropes, away from the fire where they will collect a new supply of smoke, ash, and dirt.

After a full day of walking in the outdoors, it feels great to quit early, wash, and lie in the late afternoon sun.

GARBAGE

What you cannot eat, burn; if it will not burn, pack it and take it out. Many areas have too much traffic to bury garbage, and, what the animals do not dig up, the frost heaves up. It is pointless to travel many miles to a wilderness setting only to camp in your own, or someone else's, garbage. If you can carry it in, you can carry it out.

Used cans should have both ends removed, and the entire can burned. Any excess food will be burned off. Crush the cans with your boot and pack in a designated plastic bag.

Before leaving your site, pick through your soaked fireplace for bits of foil, staples, metal caps, etc. Plastic bags and bottles release toxic fumes while burning.

Garbage, because of its fumes and unattractive odor, should be burned after dinner, for obvious reasons. You may consider this elementary but a lot of people find out by experience.

Treat the outdoors with respect, and you will enjoy it more and enjoy it longer. Let's all do a little more than our share in protecting the wilderness environment.

Safety: Avoiding Trouble 17

COMMON SENSE
ACCIDENT PREVENTION

After reading this chapter, you may think that camping in isolated country involves moving from one disaster to the next. With a measure of common sense prevention, wilderness camping is actually very safe. It is true that someone in your group may nick a finger with a knife, or burn a hand picking up a hot skillet, or sprain an ankle while climbing. These are minor accidents, requiring attention, but not life-or-death situations.

Most minor and major accidents can be avoided. Think twice before acting — about rapids you want to shoot, the cliff you want to scale, the steep hill you want to ski, the water you want to drink. No one is more aware of the risks of the situation than you.

If you plan to camp in uninhabited regions, have the knowledge and skills of basic first aid. Knowledge lies in understanding what is happening and what to do. Skill is the ability to do what needs to be done. A Red Cross or St. John's Ambulance first-aid handbook is a good place to start; enrolling in a night-school class on first aid is another step in the right direction. A first-aid class will teach you what to do in case of cuts and scrapes, severe bleeding, burns, simple and compound fractures, and how to apply artificial respiration.

THE FIRST-AID KIT

Always carry a small first-aid kit to handle minor cuts and burns. The kit should be packed where it can be reached quickly. It is a good idea to spray paint the kit or tape some luminescent color to it so that it will be easier to spot in the dark.

My kit includes a small box containing a dozen salt tablets, aspirins, and codeine tablets. Since working releases salt through the pores of the skin, the body develops a need for an increased intake of salt. This need is intensified in hot weather. Salt tablets help reduce heat exhaustion. The aspirins are for headaches, toothaches, and minor pain. Codeine tablets are used in case of severe pain. Explain to your doctor why you want the codeine, and he will provide you with a prescription. Fortunately, no one, on any of the trips I have been on so far, has needed it. A used 35-mm. film case makes a handy pill bottle.

A tensor bandage has a thousand uses; many of them have nothing to do with first aid, but if it is clean, it is useful for sprains, severe cuts, as an arm sling, and even for binding splints.

Take a needle and thread. There is always a button that pops off, a pant crotch that splits, or a pack strap that tears. Also, there is the remote possibility a wound may have to be stitched. (This should only be attempted if taping the wound closed has failed.)

A kit such as this weighs only a few ounces but contains all necessary items to handle most minor accidents. Some campers prefer larger kits — fine, provided the extra items are not in place of basic first aid knowledge.

A BASIC FIRST AID KIT

12 salt tablets
12 aspirins
12 codeine tablets
1 3-inch tensor bandage
1 needle and thread
4 sterile gauze pads
1 tube of antiseptic cream
6 bandages
1 1/2-inch roll of adhesive tape
1 1-inch roll of gauze bandage

A basic first aid kit. The little match box contains salt tablets, aspirins, and codeine tablets.

BLISTERS

Blisters give warning signals, whether on a palm rubbed by a paddle, or a heel irritated by a shoe. You *can* prevent the blister from becoming ugly. Take a minute, and stop the whole group for a rest. Tape the tender spot with adhesive and you are ready to travel again. Plastic bandages work loose and leave the budding blister to develop, so use adhesive tape. If you decide not to stop, you will be in pain for the rest of the trip. Note that blisters develop on the heels during uphill climbs and on the toes during downhill hikes. Forewarned is forearmed.

SUNBURN

Our culture associates tanned skin with youth and health. In an effort to attain a golden skin, more than one pink body has been overcooked and turned into a painful, red beet. Use the buddy system to prevent overdoing a good thing — "I'll watch your back if you watch mine." Keep in mind the famous last words "Oh, I never burn, I just brown." But don't rub it in the next morning when the packs are pulled on. On the other hand, don't offer a lot of sympathy either.

ROCK AND SNOW SLIDES

Last summer while hiking near Lake Louise, Alberta, I saw a small avalanche for the first time. Since most of my camping had been in the east, avalanches to me were a new phenomenon. The roar of rock and snow echoed through the whole valley. The avalanche tore through trees like a hand sweeping chess men from a board. A broken forest of split trees was left in its wake. The thunder of the avalanche hung in the air for a few seconds after the last rock stopped and the last tree had broken.

Since then, I have become sensitive to the danger of a rock or snow slide. Any slope with an angle of 30° or more can become a slide. Some slides are triggered by no more than a loud sound, others are started by hikers crossing the slide zone.

Snow slides tend to occur on slopes that undergo wide temperature changes. An avalanche is more likely after a crusty layer of snow is topped by a new layer of light soft snow. The wind, a sharp noise, or a rise or drop in air temperature could start it to slide.

Before hiking into mountainous regions, ask at a conservation or park office for known areas of potential slides. Watch for areas where the trees have been damaged by previous slides. Avoid these areas as much as possible.

MOUNTAIN SICKNESS

A rapid increase in altitude is a severe strain on one's body. The body has difficulty maintaining its constant need for oxygen at the increased altitude, and so the body's oxygen level drops. New physical stresses are placed on the body which demand more than the usual amount of oxygen; stresses such as exertion in walking and skiing, exposure to wind, dry air, cold or heat, and bright sunlight.

The body usually responds first at the stomach. A nauseous feeling, with weakness and dizziness, is usually the first symptom of mountain sickness. Other symptoms are headaches and insomnia. It is not uncommon for only one or a combination of symptoms to strike the unwary camper.

When mountain sickness hits you, take it easy. Eat less and scatter your munching throughout the day. Plenty of fluids will replace the moisture lost through sweat and breath into dry mountain air. The body also may need a little extra salt. During the night, even if sleep seems impossible, lie still and try to relax. The rest alone will help.

The best way to prevent mountain sickness is by doing strenuous exercises before entering the mountains. Getting fit will develop the respiratory and cardiovascular systems and reduce the altitude's strain on the body. Once in the mountains, gradually increase the amount of activity over the first few days, and watch for the first warning symptoms.

HYPOTHERMIA

Hypothermia, or exposure as it is commonly called, occurs when the body cannot maintain its internal temperature. When the central cavity, where the major organs are situated, drops to about 27°C (80°F), death follows. The body does not freeze; hypothermia can occur in temperatures well above freezing. Improper clothing, wet clothing, and windy weather, all contribute to the body's difficulty in maintaining its internal temperature. If someone has got wet and the weather is cold, watch for symptoms of hypothermia. The victim feels tired; his speech is slurred and sometimes incoherent. Other symptoms are poor coordination, slow pulse and breathing, dilated pupils. The victim will appear somewhat "stoned." He must be kept as warm as possible. Wrap him in a sleeping bag and feed him hot fluids. Drinks containing sugar, such as hot chocolate, produce energy that the body can put to work quickly. Because of impaired reasoning, the victim may believe there is nothing wrong. Shivering may follow — the shakes. It is not a sign that the danger of hypothermia is past, so keep him warm.

143

To avoid hypothermia, keep your clothing dry (if it gets wet, put on dry clothing or build a fire); at the first signs of becoming cold, put on more layers and build a fire to warm up. Boil some water and drink hot fluids.

FROSTBITE

Frostbite gives a warning signal. It first turns red, then changes into a white patch. Later, blisters may appear followed by peeling. It occurs most commonly on feet, hands, and, especially, the face and ears. The body sacrifices the farthest skin areas to keep the central cavity at its normal temperature. Whether or not you get frostbitten depends on wind velocity, duration of exposure, and insulating ability of clothing. The skin first feels cold and is crisp to touch. Soon, the cold feeling leaves and the skin feels numb — a sign that the skin is frozen. Do not rub it, but place a warm dry towel, scarf, or blanket over the area. I have trouble with my nose. It freezes very quickly and since I cannot see it, I count on the buddy system. As redness sets in, I cover it with my warm hand and allow it to heat the frozen skin. Usually I can save it before it freezes enough to blister.

The best prevention is to keep the body warm and to wear extra socks or mitts for those areas that you find get cold quickly.

For your face, a thick layer of vaseline helps, but if it is really cold, a face mask may be needed.

FREEZING

First, the skin becomes frostbitten; then freezing can set deeper into the flesh. In its frozen state, the skin is painless and has a yellowish tint. It takes on a waxy feel and loses its flex, but it does not become brittle. To prevent blisters, you must warm it as soon as practical. If possible, place the area into warm (not hot) water. Otherwise, lay your warm hand over the area and cover the area with a blanket. Thawing is slow and painful. Give the person warm fluids but no alcohol and put him in a warm sleeping bag. If it is available, set him into a warm bath of around 45°C (112°F). Watch for signs of hypothermia.

Be sure you are wearing adequate boots, mitts, and clothing. Remember that frostbite strikes first. Take its warning seriously and put on extra clothing. Build a fire and warm your face, hands, and feet at the redness stage, before the freezing process can begin.

LUNG FROSTBITE

Heavy exercise in extreme temperatures (-30°C or -22°F) can damage the membranes in the lungs. Running, skiing, or hard work may allow the cold air to burn the lungs. The lungs react by bleeding and asthmatic breathing: the victim will spit up blood. Stop what you are doing and cover the mouth and nose with your hand or scarf. This will force you to rebreathe warm air, and your lungs will heal in a day or so.

SNOW BLINDNESS

Ultraviolet sun rays do not create glare but they do enter the eyes. In strong doses, such as on sunlit snow, they can burn the back of the eyes. There is no warning and the symptoms appear two to 12 hours later — the eyes become painful with a burning feeling. Headaches and depression often follow. In the course of one to 5 days, the symptoms gradually disappear. Wear sun glasses before the sun can do any damage.

THIN ICE

Always check the thickness of ice before walking on it. Cut a hole with your knife to check that it is at least three inches thick. I always carry some rope when I cross frozen streams and lakes. The rope can be used for a quick rescue.

If you do fall through, spread your legs and thrash your arms like crazy. The thrashing will improve body circulation. In very cold water such as in the arctic, the temperature shock may stop the heart. If it does not, the victim has only a few minutes before hypothermia kills him. You have a good chance with your clothes on as insulation. As soon as you get out, strip, and build a fire. Drink plenty of hot fluids and dress in warm, dry clothing. Watch for signs of hypothermia.

Uninvited Wildlife 18

To glimpse animals in their natural habitat is one of the greatest rewards of wilderness camping. The excitement of stalking wild grouse or sighting a moose with her calf are memories treasured for many years to come. Occasionally the camper will have a face-to-face encounter with a creature of the wilds. Usually these meetings are brief and delight the camper. From time to time, however, an unfortunate incident does occur. The wilderness camper must know how to deal with it.

LITTLE TROUBLEMAKERS

In the outdoors, there are numerous small mammals that observe your eating habits and look for scraps. I once returned to a plate of freshly filleted bass to watch a fat raccoon scurrying away with the meatiest fillet. An acquaintance of mine was nibbling on soda crackers in bed one evening. Tiny crumbs fell inside his sleeping bag and worked their way to his feet. In the morning, he found that his sleeping bag had become "holey"; the hungry mice and most of the crumbs were gone. By keeping food properly packed at all times, you can avoid these annoying inconveniences.

Fresh meat should be slung from a tree far above the ground and well below the tree branches to prevent hungry animals from raiding your stock.

Keep your campsite clean and you will avoid unwanted encounters. I recall one amusing story, when my brother Rick spent a night near an overturned garbage can. Very wisely, or so he thought, he scooped up the mess and firmly pressed the lid on, sacked in, and fell asleep gazing at the starry sky. In the night, he woke and looked down at his feet. Sitting on his lap and staring up at him, was a little skunk. "You rat," said the skunk, through his stare, "you swiped my supper and now I will pay you back." Rick froze solid and began to dream of a tomato juice bath for breakfast. Fortunately, the little guy showed mercy and sauntered away.

The slow porcupine can also be a troublemaker. His special treat is salt, and, since he enjoys wood as well, you had better keep your paddles and hatchets tucked safely away during the night.

BEARS

Because of television cartoons and stuffed toys, we have developed an image of the bear as friendly, easygoing, and cuddly. But bears are not domesticated; they are wild animals, occasionally unpredictable. Bears in the far wilds are afraid of man, and they will avoid a confrontation.

Black bears, which are sometimes brown, are seldom interested in you, but they may be attracted to your supplies. Semi-tame fellows become particularly bold in protected parks. Sometimes they become so bold that they tear tents and smash coolers looking for fresh food. When you are camping in such areas, keep all your food tightly packed and slung from trees. If you meet a snooping black bear, bang on pots and yell your head off; he'll be so frightened he'll take off like a shot.

The giant grizzly and his cousin the Alaskan Kodiak are moody and can become very aggressive even when not provoked. When you are traveling in the western United States, Canada, or Alaska look ahead and watch for fresh bear tracks or droppings.

I recall an experience when camping in the Rockies. Before settling down for the night, I urinated on some nearby animal trails, thinking that if a bear did come along, at least he would be warned of my presence. It worked — at least I saw no signs of bears.

If you ever come across a mean grizzly who decides to chase you despite your yelling and banging tactics, climb the nearest tree. Grizzlies do not climb. Black bears do, so make sure you know the difference. Bears are faster runners than you for short distances, so pick a tree quickly. If by some misfortune, a bear begins to maul you, play dead and lie on your stomach. Apparently this trick works, but I hope never to have to test it.

THE MOOSE

A bull moose is one of the most spectacular of wild creatures. If you spot one, observe from a distance. Occasionally during mating season and while a cow has a calf, they can be aggressive. While in Fort Albany, Ontario, a Cree woman told me a story of two white duck-hunters who came upon a swimming bull. They lassoed his antlers and tied the rope to the bow of their boat. The little outboard was no match for the moose, and, when he got his feet on land, he took off for the cover of the bush. The men jumped out in time, but the boat was smashed. The hunters were lucky.

RABIES

Rabies is a viral infection that can be transmitted to other mammals via saliva through a bite. It spreads fastest among animals that live in dens. Foxes, skunks, bats, and rabbits spread the disease rapidly. A diseased animal will have no fear of man; it will look sick and it will appear lost. In the disease's late stages, the animal may be frothing at the mouth. If you see such an animal, avoid it and report the incident to the nearest conservation authority as soon as you can. If bitten, waste no time getting to a hospital. If possible kill the animal and take it to a veterinarian. He will ascertain if the animal was indeed rabid. The treatment is a series of painful shots in the stomach, but it is a better alternative than death.

SNAKES

These ugly creatures play an important role in nature's food chain. If you do get bitten, induce bleeding and go to a hospital. If you camp in areas where snakes are common (such as in the southwestern United States) carry a snakebite kit or an anti-venom kit. Your doctor is the best person to advise you on an anti-venom kit. He may be able to set one up for you and explain how to use it. A snakebite kit is

149

simpler. It is based on the principle of sucking out the poison. Some sporting goods stores carry them in snake areas. Again, I advise a discussion with your doctor. He can tell you which is best.

THE PLAGUE OF THE NORTH

Blackflies and mosquitoes are the biggest enemy of the wilderness camper. Blackflies peak in numbers and ferocity shortly after a warm spell in the spring. Mosquitoes soon follow. Often I plan my trips in early spring before the leaves are out just as the lake ice melts or in late summer to avoid these pests.

The best defense is to dress in bulky clothing with a tight weave. Sleeve cuffs must fit snugly and pant legs should be tucked into socks or boots. Avoid light colored clothing. Mosquitoes are less attracted to dark colors. Perfumes and sweet-smelling lotions also attract these fellows.

The best insect repellent contains N — N-diethyl-m-toluamide. Buy the commercial repellent that has the highest percentage of this compound. Or, go to a drug store and the pharmacist can sell you the ingredients to mix your own. Dilute it in an alcohol base. Insect lotions or jellies stay on your skin longer than aerosols, but with an aerosol you can spray your pant and sleeve cuffs. Your diet can also attract insects. Eating bananas releases a skin odor that attracts insects while citrus fruits repel them. If you do not have repellent with you, rub a grapefruit or orange peel on your skin.

During bug season, pick a campsite that will have a breeze and, if need be, stand in the smoke for relief. Keep in mind that mosquitoes breed in stagnant water and blackflies breed in running water. During these battles, it is encouraging to remember that at night you can close up the netting, kill the few that slipped in, and enjoy the retreat.

GIANT FLIES

Repellents are useless against horseflies and deerflies. I once set up a smoking PIC and they used it as a landing base. They seem to like bare backs, so wear loose clothing at all times.

150

NO SEE'UMS

One summer six of us were paddling to Moose Factory on James Bay. We stopped late to set up camp. Earlier in the day it had rained, then it had become very warm. Our campsite bordered a large grassy area. While setting up our tents, tiny "no see'ums" struck us in hordes. These insects, smaller than a period (.), crawled on to our warm skin. Their nips gave a lousy, itchy feeling all over. We scrambled into our sleeping bags taking a hundred guests with us. During the night the itching stopped, as the air temperature fell.

If you have never met these bugs, you will understand our experience only after they surprise you. Fortunately, their bites are not serious, only uncomfortable.

For any insect bites, calamine lotion helps reduce the swelling and relieve the itch. Baking soda made into a thick paste or even clean mud smeared over the bites brings some relief. Some people build up a tolerance for insect bites and the swelling and itchy sensation heal rapidly. Others do not. Perhaps you may be lucky, but don't count on it. Remember, the best defense is clothing.

TICKS

Ticks live on vegetation and sometimes crawl on to clothing. They move to bare skin, usually the back of the neck. There, they give a painless bite and begin to feed on your blood. If you tear the tick off, the head could be left embedded in the skin, and infection could result. A better way is to burn them off with a hot coal or cigaret, or, cover the entire insect with a thick lotion or vaseline. They soon suffocate and fall off.

WASPS, YELLOWJACKETS, AND BEES

If you have never been stung by a wasp, hornet, or bee, you should find out if you are allergic to their venom. Consult your doctor and, if you are allergic, he can give you some medication to take in case you are bitten. Usually doctors will advise an antihistamine with some adrenalin.

While camping, keep your eyes open. Hornets live in the ground, so wear shoes. By mistake, some buddies once set their tent on top of

POISON IVY

a nest. Going into the tent, I picked up a couple of yellowjackets under my shirt. I was jumping around inside the tent like a stone in a hub cap. Like mosquitoes, perfumes, sweet lotions, and bright colors attract all these buzzing stingers.

Wasps and hornets can sting a couple of times, but bees lose their stinger in the wound. As the stinger rests, it continues to release venom. If you attempt to pick it out with tweezers or fingers, you will squeeze more venom into the wound. Use the blade of a knife or even a finger and scrape across the skin to remove the stinger. To any of these stings, apply a cool compress and a baking soda paste if available. You may wish to add baking soda to your first-aid kit.

POISONOUS PLANTS

Poison ivy, oak, and sumac release a toxic chemical from their sap. In spring and early summer, the sap is at its most volatile. These plants are sun loving and grow in open areas near trees. Most people pick up the sap from walking through the plants and then handling their boots and pant legs. Some people have been infected by their dogs after the dog has been roaming through a patch. Learn to recognize the plant, and watch for it.

If infected, a redness will appear almost immediately. Later, an itchiness will develop, and, if infected seriously enough, water blisters form. If you think you are infected, wash immediately with a strong soap, rinse, and repeat. Hot compresses help to relieve some of the itching. Scratching may bring on infection. If the symptoms continue, consult your doctor.

153

Survival   19

This chapter is meant to be read but never applied. Using common sense, careful planning, and safe camping, the wilderness camper should never find himself in a live-or-die situation. Unfortunately, sometimes an error is made. It could be an act of God, but is usually a wrong decision. Many parts of the North American wilderness are extremely isolated. A knowledge of basic survival techniques can make the difference between never being found and coming out alive.

A faddish trend in camping has developed toward it becoming a survival-simulated exercise. Schools of survival camping have conducted theoretical classes, then entered the wilds to apply their skills. This frontier experience is gained at the cost of hacked trees, ripped vegetation, and destroyed wildlife. The principles of survival camping generate a conquering attitude — one lives in spite of the wilderness, not in harmony with it.

Many campers who dream of seeing a moose in its natural habitat tear up the feeding grounds looking for wild edible plants; then ask where the moose have gone.

One can take this point to an extreme. After all, the odd fresh pickerel, a small watercress salad, or some blueberry bannock add immensely to the wilderness experience. Use your common sense and respect the wilds.

One book cannot describe all the survival techniques. Much depends on your circumstances; people in a plane grounded in the Yukon need different skills than those lost in a desert.

155

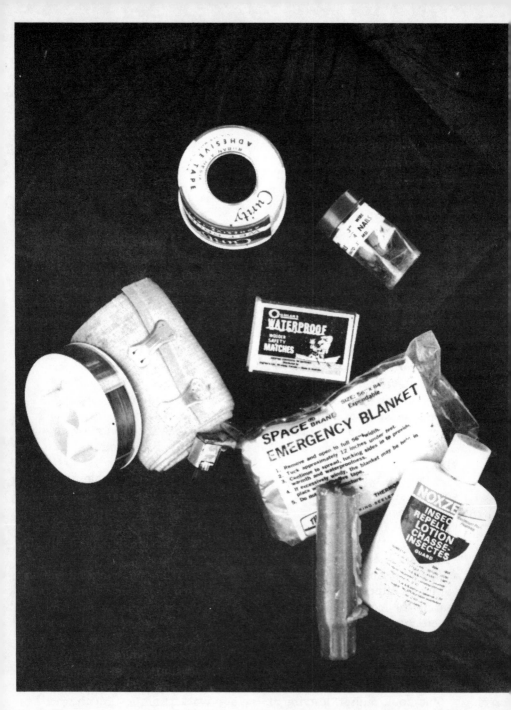

A simple survival kit. A compass, while not in the photo, is an essential. The bottle labelled "nails" contains a dozen fishhooks.

HYPOTHERMIA: THE NUMBER ONE ENEMY

In most survival situations, there exists only one major danger — hypothermia or exposure. First, reduce the loss of body heat and moisture to the air. If you are stranded in the desert, first cover yourself from the sun. If you are trapped by a snowstorm, the cold is your enemy. Food and water are secondary considerations: temperature extremes are the killers.

No matter where you go in the back country, you should always carry a small package of waterproof matches and a knife. With these two items, you will be able to survive most wilderness accidents.

Imagine for a moment, that because of a freak accident, you have become lost without equipment in an isolated area. Perhaps your plane has crashed, then burned; your canoe has overturned and has been swept away; or, while hiking, you wandered from your campsite and got lost. You are lightly dressed, you have your waterproof matches, a knife, and your arm is hurt. You should be able to come out alive. First, attend to your arm. If it is bleeding, make a bandage from a piece of your clothing. Tie it firmly in place. If it is broken, make a simple splint from birchbark padded with moss. (The bark may need to be reinforced with sticks.) After you have taken care of your injury, your next concern is to maintain your body heat.

If you are wet or getting cold, build a fire to dry out and warm up. You may wish to cut some soft hemlock boughs and stuff them into your shirt or even your pant legs. Build up a good supply of firewood.

If it is not already dark, it soon will be, and your body will be seeking sleep. You must protect your precious body heat by building a shelter. If the shelter is near an open area, such as a frozen lake, or bare hillside, you will be more easily spotted from a plane. If on a canoe trip, build your shelter near the water where you may be seen by other canoe-trippers moving along the river.

There are many places to build your shelter: against the trunk of a downed tree, under the low branches of a large tree, or against the root structure of an overturned tree. In winter you can dig a shelter out of a snowbank. In front of your shelter, build a small fire with reflector logs packed with mud. This will provide valuable heat while you are sleeping or resting.

A simple lean-to can be built with no tools.

To make your bed, cut plenty of hemlock boughs or other soft evergreen branches. Lay down a 6-inch mattress with about an 8-inch top. If, during the night you get cold, heat some large stones, and bury them in the ground beneath your bed. Sleep lengthwise opposite the fire and reflector, and keep plenty of firewood within easy reach during the night. Toss on more wood as the fire gets low. The shelter will break the wind and the fire will provide needed heat. Your first night should be reasonably comfortable.

The next day, improve your new home by sealing its roof with overlapping branches, bark, moss, and mud. If you have a tarp, rainproofing is easy. The point is to set up a comfortable, warm, dry spot for a stay of at least a few days. Your need for water can wait, and you will probably be found by the time the need for food becomes critical. In fact, people have survived very well without food for over forty days; without shelter, they would not have lasted one night.

If you find yourself in a situation without a knife or matches, follow the same procedure as above. Branches will need to be torn from the trees rather than cut. You may be able to start a fire with a lens from a pair of glasses.

WATER

After you have made an adequate shelter, look for water. In Canada and the northwestern United States, water is easily found. So, unless you are in a very arid area, water should not be a serious problem. Water flows downhill, so the best places to seek it are at the bottom of gorges and valleys. You also have a fair chance of finding water by digging at the base of cliffs, rock piles, or depressions in rolling land. Another place in which you can dig is in dried riverbeds at the base of outside curves in the river.

CALLING FOR HELP

With a comfortable shelter and a supply of water, a stranded camper can survive reasonably well for up to, or even longer than, one month. Now focus your attention on calling for help. During the daylight hours, a steady signal of spiraling smoke can be seen for miles. During the night, a bright light such as a flare is best, but a large fire is better than nothing. There is no reason to keep a large fire going at night, unless you hear an airplane.

It is best to keep your fire burning slowly all day and have a supply of green brush to create a lot of smoke. Use a shiny object such as a mirror, belt buckle, bottom of a tin can, or knife blade to reflect the sun. When you hear a plane, signal with sun and smoke.

If you are waiting near the bank of a large river, place something at the bank to capture the attention of anyone passing by. The object should attract attention, such as a bright red scarf, for example.

If you are near a frozen lake, lay dark branches in the shape of, or, stamp out, a giant S.O.S. signal in the snow. Such signals are much easier to spot from the air.

159

With your signals ready, sit and wait. To attempt to walk out without a compass is to invite suicide. With miles of bush or rocky country, you are sure to stay lost without your precious shelter. You are far safer to wait even if you are sure of the exact route out. Also, if you are moving around, the chances of a search party finding you are reduced.

SURVIVAL KIT

While camping in isolated country, waterproof matches and a knife never leave my body. I keep careful track of my compass and never leave it behind. I also carry a small survival kit in a plastic bag tucked in the outside pocket of my knapsack. This kit holds only a few items but each item can be used in a variety of survival situations: the candle to aid fire building in damp weather as well as to provide some light during the night; the "space" blanket is similar to a large sheet of strong foil and can be used as a ground sheet, as the roof of a shelter, or, if it is very cold, as a blanket to reduce heat loss by radiation and air convection; the fishing line can be used as string to tie the shelter roof, to make animal snares, or for fishing; the little bottle labelled "nails" contains about twelve fish hooks; the tensor bandage can be used for bandaging, tying, or making mitts, socks, and ear protectors; the butane lighter will light even when still slightly wet. Its adjustable flame is not easily blown out by the wind and would make signal fire lighting very quik.

MY SURVIVAL KIT

1. Silva compass with a magnifying glass
2. Waterproof matches
3. Short candle
4. "Space" blanket
5. Spool of fishing line
6. Twelve fishing hooks
7. Three-inch tensor bandage
8. Butane lighter
9. Pocket knife

160

FOOD

When you are safe from the danger of exposure, you can start to scrounge for food.

Meat

Fishing in summer or winter offers the best returns on your hunting efforts. Animal snares made of fishing line or shoelaces along trails may bring results. Summer insects such as ants, beetles, grasshoppers, etc., can be collected and eaten raw or lightly fried. Insects contain a lot of nourishment: just look at the size of some black bears. Birds of any species and their eggs are edible. Fish eggs, crawfish, salamanders, lizards, and snakes also make good eating. You may be fortunate enough to surprise a slow-moving porcupine. He cannot throw his quills, so you can club him with a large stick.

I have read in several survival books that animal snares can be made of fishing line or shoelaces. A simple noose, a loop with a slip knot, is hung over the animal's trail. The idea is that the game moves through the loop and is snared. But unless you know exactly what you are doing, it is doubtful that your efforts will be fruitful.

Plants

Many wild plants are acrid and unpalatable when raw. Getting rid of the acrid juices by boiling the plants in two or three sets of water greatly improves their flavor. Most of the plants are tender in the spring; by the time they have reached full bloom they have become tough and bitter. You will recognize immediately many of the plants listed. Memorize a few for an emergency situation. You may wish to get hold of a field guide handbook to look up the ones with which you are not familiar.

STEMS AND LEAVES

Dandelion: Boil the leaves in two lots of water to remove the bitterness. Serve like spinach. Very young leaves can be eaten raw in a green salad.
Chicory: This bulbous, flowering plant grows in woodsides and in fields. All the parts of chicory can be eaten. The young leaves are especially tasty in a salad.
Watercress: This popular salad green grows near rapid streams.

161

Milkweed: The very young shoots are good only in the spring. Cooking the young seed pods produces a tasty dish.

Ferns: People throughout the world find the budding fiddleheads of ferns a delight. The young stems must be curled in a fiddlehead. As the plant matures, it becomes poisonous. In their infancy, ferns can be eaten raw or be boiled lightly like asparagus. They are tender and delicious.

Burdock: The great burdock is easier to prepare than the smaller variety. The tender roots can be peeled and boiled in salted water. They can be eaten boiled or fried. After mashing the boiled roots, you can make cakes. The young leaves can be eaten as greens and the young leaf stalks can be skinned and enjoyed raw.

Clover: Before the plant flowers, dip the young plants into salted water and eat as greens.

Nettles: Collect the leaves and small entire plant with gloves to prevent stinging from their tiny fuzz. Boiling removes the stinging and leaves a mild flavored broth. Thicken and flavor soup or, eat as a spinach. Nettles are a good source of minerals and Vitamins A and C.

Cattail: Cut into the inner stem to about one foot above the ground. The tender core can be eaten raw or boiled.

Sorrel: This plant is a tasty alternative to rhubarb. Boil the leaves and stems and add sugar (if available).

Lichens: Boil, dry, then pound the lichen into a powder. The powder can be used as a soup thickener, gravy base, or as seasoning for stews.

ROOTS AND SEEDS

Evening Primrose: The roots in their first year before the plant blossoms are edible. Boiling them in two changes of water gives them a subtle nutty flavour.

Arrowhead: The plant grows in water or very wet areas. The roots can be boiled and taste a little like stewed potatoes with a light chestnut flavor.

Silverweed: Sometimes called "goosegrass," it grows along the shores of marshes and ponds. The roots can be baked or boiled. They taste like parsnips.

Wild Rice: Rice takes a long time to prepare. Dry out the unripened seeds and then parch them for a half-hour over low heat. Allow the

162

seeds to cool, then hull and wash the parched seeds. Cook in soups, with meat, or as plain rice.

Sunflower: The seeds can be dried and eaten or pounded into flour.

Yellow Birch: The bud can be eaten raw in the late winter. The sap can be boiled into a syrup in early spring. Tea can be made from the leaves.

FRUITS

Remember some general rules about berries: i) Blue or black colored berries are generally safe to eat if they are *not* growing in clusters; ii) red berries are usually unsafe; unless you are absolutely certain of their identity, white berries should be left on the plant.

Wild raspberries, blueberries, and strawberries are common favorites. You may not be familiar with crowberries, partridge berries, and service berries. Look them up in your field guide to add variety to your next trip.

MUSHROOMS

Many mushrooms are poisonous so proper identification must be made. Since they contain little food value, eating them is seldom worth the risk.

BEVERAGES

Staghorn Sumac: A fruit-ade can be made from the red fruit of the dwarf sumac. Boil the fruit, then strain out the remains. Add sugar and enjoy the syrup. There are poisonous sumacs; so take care.

Sassafras Tea: Pioneers used to boil the roots into a tea. Add sugar and enjoy.

Sap: Late winter and early spring is best for collecting sap. The excess water can be boiled off to leave a sweet, nutritious drink. Maple, basswood, poplar, and birch are good sources. Between the wood and bark of the pine and poplar, one can find a gooey pulp. It can be eaten or chewed like gum.

Other beverages can be made from pine needles, birch leaves, wintergreen, peppermint, and spearmint.

Appendix I: Bush Tent

This bush tent weighs 6½ lbs. and is roomy enough for two or, occasionally, three. It costs about $60. It is designed for primarily forest camping via canoe. (A backpacker may want to make a lighter tent by using a smaller design and floor pattern.)

The bush tent can be erected quickly. The floor is simply staked into the ground; the peaks can be tied to tree branches or to a rope slung from trees. In case there are no trees, a straight 6-ft.-pole or even a paddle set on a rock will keep the tent erect. Erected in this manner, our tent has survived several violent storms without blowing over or tearing. For me, it is the perfect tent.

If you wish to make a similar tent, roll up your sleeves and get to work. First, carefully read the chapters on tents and on making your own. Following the directions in Chapter 9 on making your own, cut the pieces into the shapes listed here, and sew them together. It is easy!

1.SIDE PANEL — TWO FRONT PIECES

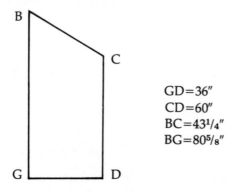

GD=36″
CD=60″
BC=43¼″
BG=80⅝″

2. SIDE PANEL — TWO MIDDLE PIECES

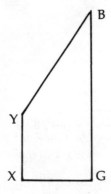

BG=80⁵/₈″
XG=35″
XY=33¹/₈″

3. SIDE PANEL — TWO REAR PIECES

AX=25″
XY=33¹/₈″

4. BACK PANELS — TWO PIECES

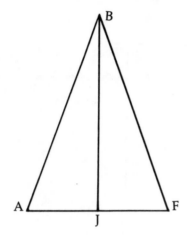

AJ=35″
JF=35″
BJ=93³/₄″

5. FRONT DOORS — TWO PIECES

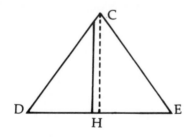

DC=CE=60″
CH=48″
DH=36″
HE=36″ (plus overlap)

Note: one panel has 3″ overlap

6. FLOOR

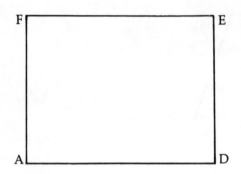

AD=8′=96″
ED=6′=72″

8′×6′

add 1″ to roll up to sides

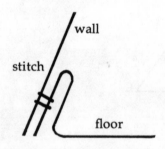

TOTAL PIECES=10 plus floor

Appendix II: Homemade Shelters

If you would like to design and make your own shelter or tent, here are some ideas that may be of interest.

1. SURVIVAL TARP

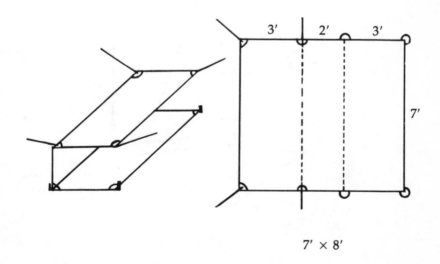

7' × 8'

2. SURVIVAL SHELTER

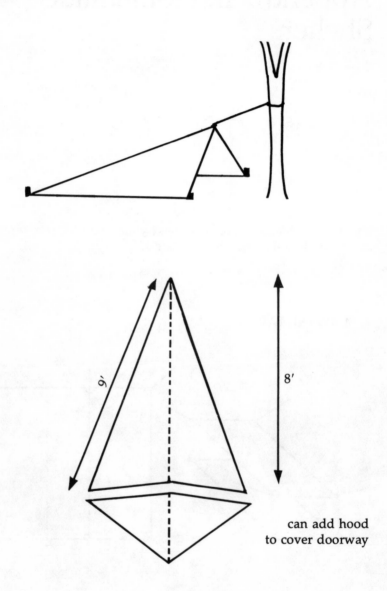

9'

8'

can add hood
to cover doorway

3. ONE MAN PUP TENT

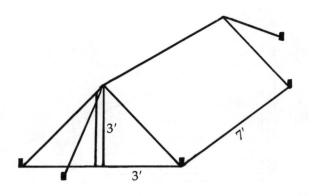

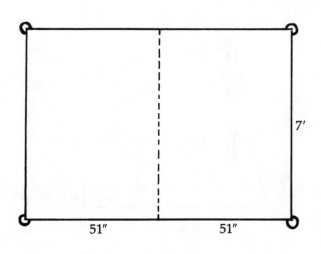

4. TWO MAN BACK TENT

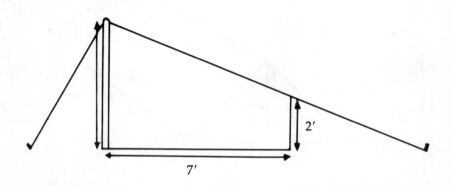

7' 2'

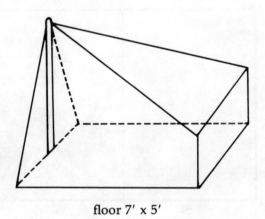

floor 7' x 5'

5. THREE MAN FOREST TENT

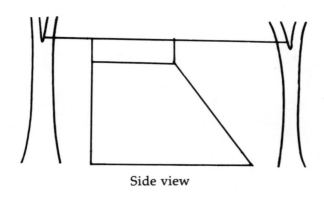

Side view

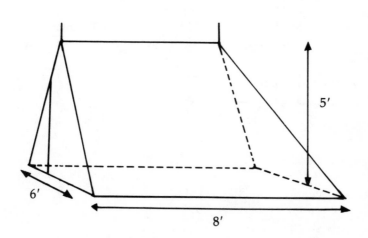

6′

8′

5′

6. FAMILY WALL TENT — FIVE MAN

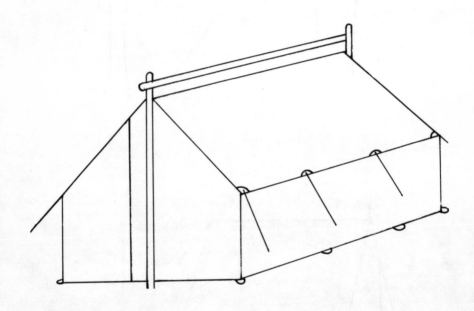

8' × 10' floor

7. FAMILY COTTAGE TENT — SEVEN MAN

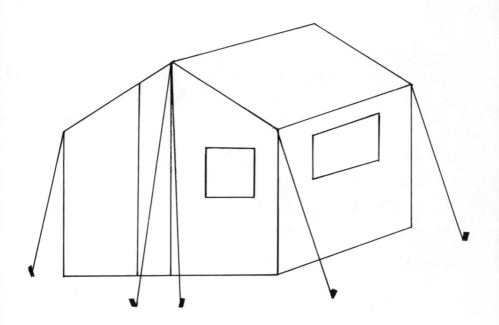

10′ × 12′ floor

Appendix III: Three Methods to Calculate Seam Lengths

In order to cut each section or piece of the tent, you must calculate the seam length first. The use of higher mathematics is not necessary, but there are three different methods, varying in mathematical complexity.

First, draw a sketch of your tent design and assign a letter to each point. It is wise not to change the letters to avoid confusion. Some lengths have to be determined by you. The floor dimensions and over-all height must be chosen, then all other seam lengths will be calculated.

Your diagram will look something like the sample diagram. Now use one of the three methods to calculate your seam lengths.

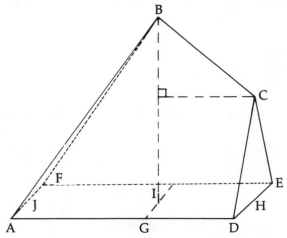

1. LAYOUT METHOD

Imagine the door on our sample tent. The base is 3 feet from the tent center to the corner (HE) and the height is 4 feet (HC). We want to know the seam length from the top of the door to the tent corner (CE).

Lay out the material on the floor and measure HE along the base and HC along the material. Be sure HC is vertical to HE by using a steel square. From the point C to the pont E will be the necessary seam length.

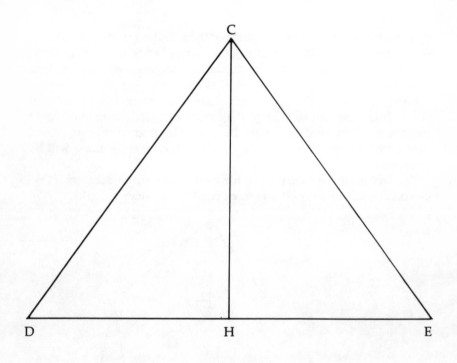

HE =3′

HC=4′

2. CARPENTER'S RULE

This method allows you to calculate all of the seam lengths without the large space necessary for the Layout Method.

Again, imagine the door on our sample tent. We want to find the length of CE. The base of the door "runs" along for 3 feet and the edge of the door "rises" 4 feet. Therefore, for every 1 foot "run" along the base, the edge "rises" 4 divided by 3, which equals 1¹/₃ feet or 16 inches.

Now, take your steel square and draw a baseline of 1 foot and a rise of 16 inches on a large piece of paper. It will look like this:

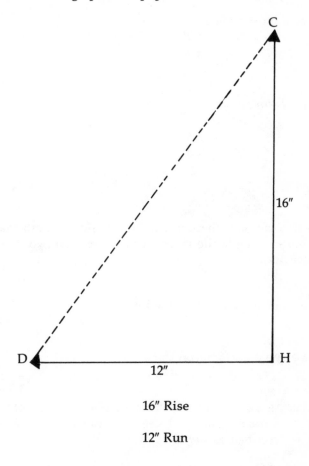

16" Rise

12" Run

The next step is to measure the dotted line between the two end-points. You should get 20 inches.

Therefore, for every 12-inch run, there will be a rise of 16 inches and a slope length of 20 inches. In the case of our door, there is

$$3 \times 12'' = 36'' \text{ run}$$
$$\text{and a } 3 \times 16'' = 48'' \text{ rise.}$$

Therefore, it must have a
$$3 \times 20'' = 60'' \text{ slope length; or}$$
$$\text{CE} = 60''$$

The door measures:
$$\text{HE} = 36''$$
$$\text{CH} = 48''$$
$$\text{CE} = 60''$$

Using this method, there is one type of slope length that creates problems. Referring to the sample tent, there exist two slopes in the large piece ABG.

BG is a slope dependent on the lines:
G1 and B1

AB is a slope dependent on the lines:
AG and BG

To calculate AB, you must first calculate the slope length of BG. This is because AB crosses planes. Once BG is calculated, use the same method as described earlier to find AB.

180

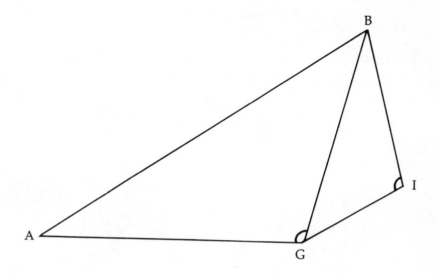

3. TRIGONOMETRIC METHOD

This method is advantageous primarily for irregular-shaped tents such as our sample tent. This method was presented to me by my good friend John Boyarchuk. It's a method of triangles which removes the problems created when slopes change planes. Some mathematical experience would be necessary for calculating the seam lengths by this method.

The basic steps are as follows:

a) Geometry

Most of the "sides" in the example tent are triangles to begin with. Only the sides ABCD and BCEF need to be broken down into triangles.

181

SIDE PANELS

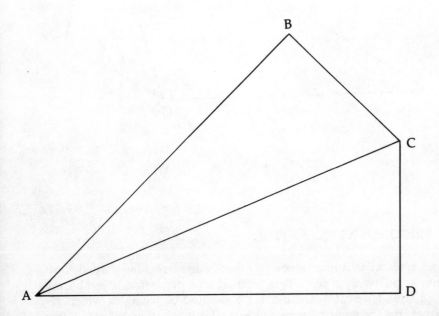

b) Point Coordinates

A three-space coordinate system is required. For our tent, we picked the point F to coincide with the origin. Refer to the diagram.

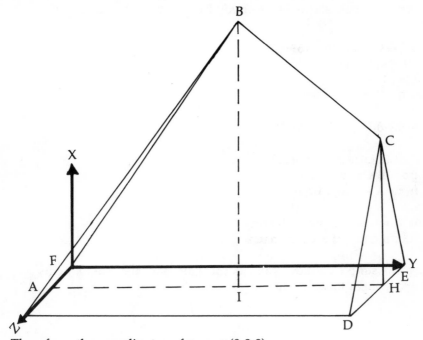

Therefore, the coordinates of F are F (0,0,0)

Point E is 8 feet along the Y axis,

> 0 feet along the X axis, and
> 0 feet along the Z axis.

Hence, E has the coordinates E (0,8,0)

Point C is 8 feet along the Y axis,
> 4 feet along the X axis, and
> 3 feet along the Z axis.

Hence, C has coordinates C (4,8,3)

The rest of the points, A,B,D,H, and I, can be determined similarly.

c) **Calculations**

Once the coordinates of all the points are determined, the distances between them can be calculated.

For example, the distance between A(0,0,6) and B(6,4,3) is denoted by AB.

$$AB = \sqrt{(6-0)^2 + (4-0)^2 + (6-3)^2}$$
$$= \sqrt{(6)^2 + (4)^2 + (3)^2}$$
$$= \sqrt{36 + 16 + 9}$$
$$= \sqrt{61} = 7.81 \text{ feet}$$

$$AB = \sqrt{(6-0)^2 + (4-0)^2 + (6-3)^2}$$

(6−0) difference of x-coordinates
"6" from B's x-coordinate
"0" from A's x-coordinate

(4−0) difference of y-coordinates
(6−3) difference of z-coordinates

Using this simple method, you can calculate all of the seam lengths and apply them to your tent.

Bibliography

Anderson, Luther A., *A Guide to Canoe Camping*. Reilly and Lee. Chicago, 1969.

Angier, Bradford. *Wilderness Cookery*. Stackpole Books. Harrisburg, Pa.

Angier, Bradford. *Survival with Style*. Stackpole Books. Harrisburg, Pa. 1972.

Angier, Bradford. *Wilderness Gear You Can Make Yourself*. Collier Books. New York. 1973.

Berglund, Berndt. *Wilderness Survival*. Modern Canadian Library. Toronto. 1974.

Berglund, Berndt and Bolsby, Clare E. *The Edible Wild*. Modern Canadian Library. Toronto. 1974.

Berglund, Berndt and Bolsby, Clare E. *Wilderness Cooking*. Charles Scribner's Sons. New York. 1973.

Berglund, Berndt. *Wilderness Living*. Charles Scribner's Sons. New York. 1976.

Bridge, Raymond. *Freewheeling: The Bicycle Camping Book*. Stackpole Books. Harrisburg, Pa. 1974.

Brunelle, Hasse. *Food for Knapsackers*. A Sierra Club Totebook. Sierra Club. San Francisco.

Herz, Jerry. *The Compleat Backpacker*. Popular Library. Toronto. 1973.

Jansen, Charles L. *Lightweight Backpacking*. Bantam Books. New York. 1974.

Jenkinson, Michael. *Wild Rivers of North America*. E.P. Dutton & Co. Inc. New York. 1973.

Johnson, James R. *Advanced Camping Techniques*. David McKay Co. Inc. New York. 1967.

Kinmount, Vikki & Axcell, Claudia. *Simple Foods for the Pack*. Sierra Book Clubs. San Francisco. 1976.

Kjellström, Bjorn. *Be Expert with Map and Compass*. New-Revised Edition. Charles Scribner's Sons. New York. 1955, 1967.

Kodet, Dr. E. & Angier, Bradford. *Being Your Own Wilderness Doctor*. Stackpole Books. Harrisburg, Pa. 1968.

Kron, Karl. *Ten Thousand Miles on a Bicycle*. University Building. Washington Square. New York. 1887.

Langer, Richard W. *The Joy of Camping*. Penguin Books Inc. Maryland. 1973.

Learn, C.R. & O'Neil, Mike. *Backpacker's Digest*. 2nd Edition. Follet Publishing Co. Chicago.

Malo, John. *Malo's Complete Guide to Canoeing and Canoe-Camping*. Revised and Updated. The New York Times Book Co. 1969. 1974.

Monk, Carl and Knap, Jerome. *A Complete Guide to Canoeing*. Pagurian Press Ltd. Toronto. 1976.

Nickel, Nick. *Nick Nickel's Canoe Canada*. Van Nostrand Reinhold Ltd. Toronto. 1976.

Knap, Jerome J. *The Complete Outdoorsman's Handbook*. Pagurian Press Ltd. Toronto. 1974.

Knap, Jerome and Alyson. *The Family Camping Handbook*. Pagurian Press Ltd. Toronto. 1975.

Saijo, Albert. *The Backpacker*. 101 Productions. San Francisco. 1972.

Thomas, Dian. *Roughing It Easy*. Warner Books. 1975.

Van Lear, Denise. Editor. *The Best About Backpacking*. A Sierra Club Totebook. Sierra Club. San Francisco.

Advanced First Aid and Emergency Care. American Red Cross. Doubleday & Co. Inc. New York. 1973.